I Used to Be
So Organized

I Used to Be So Organized

Help for Reclaiming Order and Peace

Glynnis Whitwer

LEAFWOOD
PUBLISHERS

I USED TO BE SO ORGANIZED

Help for Reclaiming Order and Peace

Copyright 2011 by Glynnis Whitwer

ISBN 978-089112-288-3
LCCN 2011021148

Printed in the United States of America

LIBRARY OF CONGRESS CATALOGING-IN-PUBLICATION DATA
Whitwer, Glynnis, 1961-
I used to be so organized : help for reclaiming order and peace / by Glynnis Whitwer.
    p. cm.
Includes bibliographical references.
ISBN 978-0-89112-288-3
1. Time management--Religious aspects--Christianity. 2. Simplicity--Religious aspects--Christianity. 3. Home economics. I. Title. II. Title: Help for reclaiming order and peace.
BV4598.5.W45 2011
640'.43--dc23
                          2011021148

Cover design by Jennette Munger
Interior text design by Sandy Armstrong

Published in association with William K. Jensen Literary Agency, 119 Bampton Court, Eugene, Oregon 97404.

Leafwood Publishers is an imprint of
Abilene Christian University Press
1626 Campus Court
Abilene, Texas 79601

1-877-816-4455
www.leafwoodpublishers.com

11 12 13 14 15 16 / 7 6 5 4 3 2 1

Dedication

I dedicate this book to my mother, M. Kathryn Sinclair Owens,
for teaching me problem solving skills at an early age,
and to all the women I've served with at Proverbs 31 Ministries.
I treasure each of you in my heart.

Table of Contents

Section One:
What Happened?

Section Two:
Finding a Balanced Approach to an Ordered Life

Section Three:
Jump-Start for the Seriously Overwhelmed

Section Four:
Simple Steps to Creating Order

Section Five:
You Can Do It!

Acknowledgments

To my husband Tod, my best friend and biggest supporter. You have lovingly tolerated all my attempts to bring beauty and order into our home. I don't know of many men who would live in a pink bedroom for years and sit on ruffled floral couches. Thank you for supporting me in God's unique design and call on my life.

To my five (teenage) blessings. I pray that someday you catch the vision for an ordered life and home, and that what seems annoying to you now (like my requests to pick up your clothes) will make sense. You bring joy to my life.

I want to honor all the women in my closest family who have modeled living a life of priorities. It doesn't always look the same, but your commitment to pursuing your passions inspires me: Mom, Helen Ann, Paula, Liz, Terry, Amy, and Tracy. I honor those women who have gone ahead of us: Both of my grandmothers (Ana Mae and Helen) and niece Christa.

Thank you to my special friends who stepped in to help with proofreading my manuscript: Beth Blake, Kathy Kurlin, Ana Stine, my mom Kathryn, and my sister Paula. Thank you all for sharing your excellent editing skills with me. Thanks also to Eileen Koff for your gift of professional mentoring, which helped prepare me to write this book.

I especially want to recognize my sisters in the faith at Proverbs 31 Ministries. Thank you especially to Lysa, Renee, and LeAnn for leading the ministry and believing in me. Thank you for seeing my unique gifting and allowing me to find a place of service alongside you. And to my precious co-laborers in ministry, too numerous to mention, your faithful obedience to Jesus spurs me on daily, and makes me better.

. . . .

Foreword

. . . . ~~~ . . . .

I remember the day I first felt *"it."* Vividly. And I can say without hesitation that I did not like the foreign feeling *at all.*

Being a put-together gal—the kind always elected to be in charge in both high school and college—I was used to being at the top of my game organizationally. Like Grandma had preached, I had "a place for everything and everything in its place." I was a stickler for scheduling, a craver of order. Managing my time well and keeping my belongings in check made me feel in control and accomplished.

So, when "it" came along, well, I was completely thrown for a loop.

What was this horrible condition that caused me to break out in hives and run for the hills? Just what was "it"? "It" was the feeling of utter disorganization, of hopelessness due not only to mess but to a messed up schedule as well. When "it" hit, it had me uttering the words I thought I'd *never* hear myself say: *"But . . . I used to be so organized!"*

Now what on earth could have happened to throw off my timing, plunging me into a downward spiral of dejection and sending me tenaciously tottering near the edge? Illness? Catastrophe? A flood or fire? Nope. Something that is very simple, really.

One morning upon arising I discovered . . . the stick turned blue!

Yes, blessed motherhood. What a privilege? What an honor. Come on, let's be real girlfriends. What a headache! Whether you became a mom by giving birth or by making the trek to bring your precious child home from the adoption agency, you all know what I'm talking about. No sooner than we lined all our ducks up in a row, along comes one of our kiddos (or their father perhaps) to knock them all down forcing us to start all over again!

But the "it" is different for everyone. Perhaps for others of you "it" is brought on by a change of employment—that fantastic new job that also takes a fantastic amount of time, time you used to have to spend on your personal life keeping things running along smoothly. Or maybe it is a relocation in residence, an ill relative, or aging parent. No matter the loop you've been thrown, you too may feel "it" craftily creeping into your formerly organized self.

Oh, how I wish years ago I'd cradled in my hands the volume you now hold. My dear friend Glynnis Whitwer knows all too well the feeling of being an in charge gal. She is truly one of the most intelligent, insightful, and capable women I know.

It will make you love her all the more when you realize she also readily admits this reality: she doesn't always have it all together. She too, as an author, a home business owner, and editor of the *Proverbs 31 Woman Magazine*, still struggles with missed appointments, lost items, and class treats that never got made. She too struggles with feelings of inadequacy, apprehension, and even sometimes fears of failure.

But Glynnis also understands a very crucial fact. She knows just where to go with her feelings of helplessness. Her encouraging words, clever ideas, and biblical insight will send you running to the only Author of perfection. Her warm, vulnerable, "I've been there" style will gently point you to the One in whom we can find our sense of worth. Not in what we accomplish each day, but in what he already accomplished at the cross.

So grab a cup of something hot and get ready to be encouraged by a girlfriend who will come along side you. Her motivating ideas will give you something to shoot for, yet her graceful and grace-filled demeanor will help you to know you aren't always going to get it all done—not all of the time.

Glynnis will help you finally strike that delicate balance between *doing* and *being*, all the while showing you how to put God and your loved ones first.

Oh sweet sister . . . you are in for a treat. Turn the page and enjoy!

Karen Ehman
Director of Speakers for Proverbs 31 Ministries; author of *The Complete Guide to Getting and Staying Organized* and *A Life That Says Welcome*; wife of twenty-five years and homeschooling mother of three.

What Happened?

Chapter One

Welcome to the New Reality

One hand gripped the steering wheel, while the other gripped the promise of multitasking efficiency. Today, I just call it my cell phone, but back in the nineties, it was a four-ounce nugget of organizational prowess.

Driving home from work that day, I marveled that I could check my phone messages remotely. Then return them. It was a modern-day miracle. That afternoon, I listened to one message after another, mentally checking items off my to-do list while driving. Satisfaction settled in my heart. Surely, I reasoned, this new tool would enable me to accomplish more than I had ever dreamed possible. I needed nothing else.

Fast-forward fifteen-plus years. I want to pat that younger, naïve me on the head. *Tsk, tsk, poor dear. She's so innocent . . . and deceived.*

It seems that the cell phone launched the beginning of something I didn't see coming. It was to be a new age, with exciting new products and promises of organizational solutions coming out every year—something innovative, something sleek—but those sparkling "somethings," when combined, would suck us all into a vortex of mind-numbing information overload and clutter unknown to generations of women before us.

My first boss was a perfect example of a different type of ordered simplicity. Fresh out of college in 1984, I found a public relations job in the office of a land developer. My bosses were a retired doctor and the wife of a doctor, who handled most of the management details. Together, they formed general and limited partnerships and built commercial buildings, medical office buildings, and retirement communities. It was a multi-million-dollar development, and Mrs. Harper organized it all on a yellow legal pad and a calendar.

No computer, e-mail, cell phone, or BlackBerry. Just a pad of paper and a pen. I reminisce about the simplicity of that time, much like my mother remembers the sweet tradition of hanging May Day baskets on the doorknobs of friends' houses. Life was simple back in the eighties. Sigh.

Now, just to manage my family's needs, I have a cell phone with unlimited texting, e-mail service on both my computer and my phone, the highest speed Internet, and a calendar hanging in my kitchen and on Outlook synced with my phone, plus a to-do list in both a spiral notebook and a project list on my computer. And I still manage to forget a dentist's appointment now and then. Don't even get me started on what it takes to manage my home-based business, work with a national ministry, write, speak, volunteer at church, and . . . oh, what? You want dinner, too?

What happened to simplicity? How did we go from needing a legal pad to organize our lives to needing seminars, the latest technological marvel, and the top ten organizing tips shouting from the headlines of every magazine on my grocery store's checkout aisles?

Electronic Technology Takeover

Unless you were born after 1980, you probably grew up in a world without much electronic technology. I actually grew up without cable and was limited to watching cartoons on Saturday morning or the occasional after-school special. My kids shudder at the horror of it.

My mind was trained to focus on one thing at a time, and there were very few interruptions in a normal day. If I was on the phone, other callers got a busy signal. If I said I was going to the store or to the library to study, I meant just that. It wasn't a chance to catch up on phone calls or check e-mail. Multitasking meant watching television while ironing.

Choices were limited as well. There were three toothpaste brands instead of ten. There were five television channels instead of five hundred. Writing a note to someone meant getting a pen. Researching a topic for a school paper meant reading *the* encyclopedia and whatever books the local library had on its shelves.

I guess it was a pretty isolated way to live. Exposure to different ways of thinking and doing things was limited for the daughter of a schoolteacher growing up in the suburbs. Yes, it was somewhat one-dimensional. But it was much simpler.

With the advent of the "car phone," as we called it, regular folks like me hopped on a technology roller coaster that seems to be speeding up. What used to be unique in the average home is now a staple. Really, I can't imagine life without all my gadgets. Nor do I want to. Yet I find life more complicated now than twenty years ago. New opportunities have opened up for me as a result of technology. Although these opportunities are wonderful, they call me to a higher level of managing my daily responsibilities.

Here's an example. In 1999, I lived in Charlotte, North Carolina, and was on staff part-time with Proverbs 31 Ministries as their newsletter editor. In the year 2000, my family moved back to Arizona. At that time, I planned to find a replacement editor and quit when I moved. After all, how could I do a job more than two thousand miles from the office?

However, God had other plans. Due to advancements in technology, I was able to continue working for Proverbs 31 Ministries from Arizona, and I have been the magazine editor since then. Our graphic designer is in North Carolina, the printer is in Alabama, and our editing team lives around the country.

In the 1990s, we managed everything through face-to-face meetings, the mail, or over the phone. We were able to bring resolution to questions and problems in one setting. Now it seems as if every decision takes longer.

Due to multiple available avenues of communication (e-mail, texting, Skype), more people are involved in discussions and decision making. I spend more time waiting for other people to get back to me than before. I'm more constrained by other people's schedules and habits than in the past. It makes life easier and harder at the same time.

Is Life Really More Complicated Now?

This new reality of interconnectedness is both a blessing and a challenge. Relationships made with co-workers, friends, and family are rich and varied. The devotions I write for Proverbs 31 Ministries are reaching women all over the world. I still marvel that a woman in South Africa or Scotland can read something I wrote and communicate with me that same day. God is weaving together his children like never before via wireless connections.

And yet, these ways of connecting to each other have created a climate of increased expectations. People expect more from me, which adds an underlying pressure to my day. People can reach me through a variety of avenues, and I'm expected to respond promptly. Some days, I find myself so busy responding to others that my priorities are neglected.

Also, as our world opens, more opportunities present themselves—personal, professional, and in ministry. More opportunities mean more decisions. Information floods in from every direction, challenging me to process it, discard the unimportant and irrelevant, and save the important. Without a solid filter for making those decisions, I find myself overcommitted and on mental overload.

Instead of frames and margins around my different responsibilities, the lines are blurred or nonexistent. Twenty years ago, I could only do my professional job in an office. Now, I can do professional work at home, home responsibilities at work, and volunteer commitments anywhere.

I'm thrilled by the possibilities one moment, then wondering how I got myself into this situation the next. Did I really say yes to that invitation? Why did I say I would write this article, staff that registration table, attend this conference, start a Facebook account, begin Twittering, etc.? There is a sense of immediacy and urgency that entraps me if I'm not careful.

The tools that were supposed to help me manage my life have actually added to the complications. Many women find themselves slaves to the master of technology instead of the other way around. We can become victims to an out-of-control schedule, information overload, and the demands of others.

Many of us feel as if someone put us in the spin cycle of the washing machine—leaving us washed up and wrung out. And then, as if that weren't enough, we got put in the dryer so things would heat up a bit.

Life can be exhausting to manage. Is it even possible to keep up, or should we just shrug our shoulders and accept a cluttered, disorganized, frustrating life?

Something Had to Change

A few years ago, I sat on my living room couch, feeling waves of panic wash through me. My chest felt weighted, my breathing shallow. Anxiety shimmered, but there was no apparent threat. However, there were looming deadlines, people expecting me to produce a variety of things, a business demanding attention, a cluttered house, hundreds of e-mails in my inbox, and a family who needed me, too.

This didn't happen overnight. My life expanded beyond my capacity to manage it over a period of about fifteen years. Technological changes weren't the only changes to my life. During that time, my husband and I had three boys through natural means and two daughters through adoption, and we moved, changed churches, and started two home-based businesses. I added book writing to my schedule and miscellaneous other projects along the way.

Something had to change. I was exhausted from setting myself up to fail and overcommitting my time. And I was sick of berating myself for not being more organized and for being unable to handle things better. I had to stop comparing myself to the "old" Glynnis who could manage life with ease. My life had changed around me, and I needed to change my practices in response.

A New Way of Thinking

It's not as if every part of my life was a disaster. Some things were working well. But some areas were so out of control that they impacted everything. I needed simplicity. I needed time to think straight. I needed to refocus my priorities. I needed more order and peace in my day.

No longer could I demand that the world around me adapt to my way of thinking. It obviously wasn't working, given my near panic attack. Unless I planned to live on an island drinking iced tea and eliminate outside responsibilities (which isn't bad, if God has called you to that way of life), I needed to find ways to manage this new reality . . . my new reality.

The truth is God has called me to an interconnected life. God has called me to minister to others. God created me to be a productive woman at work and home. God has called me to be the wife of a busy man and the mother of five.

To do all that God is calling me to do required me to find new ways to manage my life. I had to stop thinking in a one-dimensional manner and start thinking in 3-D. I had to find ways to get and keep certain controllable parts of my life in order, so I had freedom to manage the more uncontrollable parts of life.

Instead of seeing changes as inconveniences, I needed to see them as God-given ways to increase my effectiveness. I also have to know when to close doors on opportunities—or never open them in the first place.

Above all, I am on a journey to discover God's best for my life, which isn't always what I thought it would be. Although I'm a doer by nature, I have learned God cares much more about my character and the condition of my heart than the quantity or quality of my work. I'll share more about that in a later chapter.

Finding order and peace is an ongoing process, because life keeps changing. We have children. We change jobs. We move. Our children grow. Our parents' health fails. Our health changes. We get in an accident. Something is always happening to challenge us. That's why staying stuck in old patterns of organizing just doesn't work.

In this book, I hope to take you on a journey to a more ordered and peaceful life. Your journey won't look like mine because the demands on your energy and time are different. But hopefully you'll be better equipped to deal with your crazy, busy, wonderful, exciting life.

Along the journey, it is my prayer that you will draw closer to God and to discovering his purpose for your life. Life just doesn't make sense without him.

Is there an organized person in you? I believe so. She's still there. Let's go find her and bring her back together.

Chapter Two

. . . .

Information Overload

. . . . ✦ . . . .

The day I thought I was having a panic attack changed me. The constant demands left me feeling defenseless. I couldn't think straight. I couldn't process what needed to be done and when, or what I should do first.

I was on information overload with no adequate processing mechanism. The information filter I used years ago was insufficient to process the amount and type of content flowing my direction. It was like trying to strain a milkshake through a coffee filter—it wasn't flowing smoothly.

Identifying what is the most important piece of information at any given time is actually a skill you can learn. It involves dismissing the unimportant (at the moment) and narrowing your focus to what is the most critical.

My college degree was in journalism and public relations. Reporting was a foundational class for us. We learned how to separate the important information from the irrelevant so we could write an article containing what the reader needed to know. It sounds easy, but it's harder than you might think.

The first week of class, the professor wrote a list of facts on the board about a multi-car accident. The facts included details like the number of cars involved, how many police officers came, where the accident happened, and how many injuries or deaths there were. Our challenge was to identify the lead for the article. In other words, what was most important?

I don't remember the answer, but I do remember the response of the class. We couldn't figure it out. However, once the professor identified the lead for us, it was obvious. He was trained to distinguish interesting from important. During that semester, he trained us to do the same.

Why We Can't Identify the Important

Every day we face situations requiring us to separate interesting from important. We filter through buckets of facts to find the relevant ones, those that impact our decisions. Everything seems important and like a priority, making it difficult to pinpoint our own priorities and put them in order. It can be overwhelming and exhausting.

My days often feel like a circus juggling act. Just when I have a rhythm going, someone throws an apple into the mix, then a plate, a bowling pin, and a flaming torch. Soon, it's obvious I can't keep this up . . . but what do I grab and what do I let go? This is when knowing my priorities helps.

Many women stumble over the answer to this question: What are the top priorities in my life? It's a complex question, which is why the answers are elusive. In fact, I've dedicated Chapter Six to exploring this question. Once we know our priorities, it's easier to identify what to grab and what to let go until tomorrow, next week, or next year.

Instead of apples and plates, our lives are filled with hundreds of decisions. My daily decisions look something like this:

- Should I answer e-mails or start researching a class I want to teach?
- Should I watch a training video or write a devotion?

- Should I take lunch to my son at school or spend time with my mother?
- Should I balance my checkbook or write thank you notes?
- Should I stop work and spend time reading with my daughter or finish a project before dinner?

My decision-making process is often guided by:

- My energy level.
- My annoyance level.
- What is most urgent.
- Who needs me most.

At times, it's fine to respond to an urgent need based on how much energy I have. The problem is when it becomes a habit based on my inability to determine what is most important at the moment.

As purposeful women, our priorities should determine our activities. However, in our busy lives, the opposite happens: our priorities are determined by our activities. When we live an activity-driven life, we are never quite sure what's most important. When that happens consistently over time, a low level of anxiety settles in.

Information Anxiety Sets In

Have you ever felt the underlying anxiety I mentioned in the last chapter? Maybe you didn't get to the point I did with physical symptoms, but throughout your day you noticed a nagging sense of unease. This feeling is common when a person hasn't processed all the information and decisions hammering for her attention. It happens when the demands on your mental energy, attention, and time outweigh your resources to respond. As a result, low-level anxiety manifests in your life.

Mind you, these might all be good things you are facing. You might think you have no reason to be anxious. But even good things can tax your resources. Whether the decisions overwhelming you are positive or negative, most people don't know how to get to a place of peace and clarity of thought.

The problem with trying to manage all the information that swirls around us is that our brains aren't designed to capture and organize unprocessed information. David Allen, author of *Getting Things Done*, describes it like this: "The short-term-memory part of your mind—the part that tends to hold all of the incomplete, undecided, and unorganized 'stuff'—functions much like RAM on a personal computer."[1]

When too much information is left unprocessed, that underlying tension keeps us from focusing on what's really important at the moment. I'll address this concept in greater depth later in the book, but for now it's important to realize why you are having trouble getting your thoughts and life organized. There is hope and there are practical answers for you.

Information Overload and ADD

Studies are showing that information overload produces symptoms much like attention deficit disorder (ADD). Being a mom of three children with this challenge, I know what this looks like, and I have worked for years to implement systems to help them.

Psychiatrist Edward Hallowell made this observation, "[There is] a very real but unrecognized neurological phenomenon that I call attention deficit trait, or ADT. Caused by brain overload, ADT is now epidemic in organizations. The core symptoms are distractibility, inner frenzy, and impatience. People with ADT have difficulty staying organized, setting priorities, and managing time."[2]

When there is too much going on or too much stimulation, many people have an automatic response to shut down. This is especially true if they are already weakened by too much information.

Never before in history have people had to juggle as many demands on their attention as we do now. It comes at us from so many directions, and we are simply boggled by it all. Our brains struggle to keep up, but without adequate filters, we succumb to ADT.

We can trace the reasons for this auto-response to divine design. God planned for the front part of our brain to make complex decisions and for the lower part to respond to attack. Hallowell puts it this way, "This region (frontal lobes) governs what is called, aptly enough, executive functioning (EF). EF guides decision making and planning; the organization and prioritization of information and ideas; time management; and various other sophisticated, uniquely human, managerial tasks. As long as our frontal lobes remain in charge, everything is fine."[3]

The problem arises when input overloads the lower brain. Sensing danger, the survival responses activate. "Send help!" it shouts to the front brain. But the front brain is overloaded, too. "Can't!" it shouts back. Your body is shifting into crisis mode, and your executive functioning deteriorates into survival thinking, usually meaning fight or flight.

The practical application of this physiological response to information overload is to get out of that situation as fast as possible. So what happens? Here are common responses:

- Emotional overreaction
- Reckless decision making
- Lack of creativity in problem solving
- Mental flight
- Distraction techniques
- Foggy thinking
- Inability to prioritize

Is any of this sounding familiar? My guess is you have suffered through enough of this to recognize the symptoms, and you could add a few yourself.

The challenging part of information overload is that it affects all areas of your life: you can't manage your bills or your children's school papers, your closets are a mess, you're late to appointments (when you actually remember them).

I believe even the most intelligent and productive women are stymied by the overwhelming amount of data to manage. But there is hope.

Addressing Information Overload

The amount of information we must manage on a daily basis isn't going away. To succeed in our new reality, we must understand the problem and then incorporate simple daily practices to help us cope and thrive.

Identify the Problem

Disorganization is always a symptom of something else. For many, information overload is the problem. Thankfully, this isn't a physiological problem. You don't need medication to address this issue. You can make simple changes in your environment that will lead to clearer thinking and eventually more control over your time and resources.

The first step, simply enough, is to acknowledge the problem. If information overload is the issue, and your brain has reacted with primitive survival instinct, you may be blaming others for your lack of disorganization. You may blame "those kids," your spouse, or your boss. You blame your co-workers, the dog, or your bank for sending you all those statements you don't know what to do with. This type of thinking keeps you in a victim mentality, which in turn narrows your options.

While it's not your fault you don't have adequate resources to handle all the input, you are in control. So first, acknowledge there is a problem. And second, choose not to be a victim any more by making simple changes.

Put Better Filters in Place

If too much information is a root of your disorganization, then limiting what enters your mind is a foundational skill for dealing with it.

I've always loved waking up to the news. First I watched the local news from six to seven, then transitioned into the national news. My mornings were a bustle of activity as I got five children out the door for school. Even though I could handle the work (scrambling eggs and making a PB&J isn't tough), I found my anxiety level rising. I snapped at my kids over simple things, and they in turn snapped at each other.

Years earlier, I stopped letting my children watch cartoons in the morning because of the feet-dragging and arguments that happened. I wondered if I needed to apply that rule to myself.

One trial day convinced me I could survive without the news. It seems the background noise was bothering us all without us knowing it. Without the television on, we talk more, we stay more focused in gathering last-minute items, and our on-time departures have increased dramatically.

I've had to establish quiet zones in my day to keep my focus. In fact, I don't even listen to music most of the time. Even though I work at home and could blast my speakers till the windows shake, I've found it saps my mental focus. Music is reserved for times of simple work.

Create Rest Zones

Your mind needs time to rest. To the best of your ability, schedule times in your day when you can allow your mind to rest and refocus. Thinking is an underrated organizational skill. Instead of doing something all the time, you may need to think more.

For a Christian, time with the Lord can be one of those times. Take time to rest in the Lord's presence. To be productive and organized, these times with God are not just an option. Nor are they just a chance to relax after you've gotten your work done. They are a necessity to clear and purposeful thinking. But that's hard for those of us with a "Martha" personality.

Which would be me. And I don't mean Martha Stewart. No, I'm nothing like her. In fact, one Christmas I didn't even manage to decorate the tree. It got put up, and because it was pre-lit, it had lights. I managed to put a few gifts under it before Christmas—which only happened because my dear children kept looking at me with big, hopeful eyes, asking when I was going to wrap *something*. But that was it.

That Christmas ended one of the most stressful years of my life. Nothing devastating happened to my family; the demands simply exceeded my available time and energy. I was overwhelmed and in serious information overload. When that happens, I spend lots of time just trying to keep my head above water.

The Martha I'm talking about is found in the Bible, and it's *not* a flattering comparison. Luke 10 tells the story of Martha and her sister Mary. That Martha had the privilege of hostessing Jesus in her house. Instead of sitting at his feet, like her sister Mary did, Martha worked and actually complained to Jesus that Mary wasn't helping her enough.

Jesus gently chided Martha and affirmed Mary's choice to sit and spend time with him in the middle of all the work that had to be done. I remember the day clearly when I decided to follow Mary's example and sit in the middle of my mess to spend time with Jesus.

Normally, I believe everything must be clean before I can "treat" myself to some down time. I believe I have to clean the dishes, clear the counters, answer urgent e-mails, start the laundry, and check my home-based business for orders. Normally, by the time I've done all that, something else has demanded my attention, and time with Jesus is neglected—much like what happened to Martha.

But not that day. That day, I sat at the kitchen table and looked at my mess. It was big. There were papers strewn over every surface, a lunch box left on the counter from the day before, breakfast dishes everywhere, jackets from yesterday, blankets that had been left on the couch, dog fur forming balls, and the list went on. I had to fight my instinct to get up. And I won.

I sat in the middle of my mess, and I spent time with Jesus. I pictured him sitting across the table from me. It was pure pleasure . . . and the mess amazingly faded from my view. My stress melted away, and I felt renewed.

His Peace Is Available Today

That peace is available to you and me today. At any time of the day or night, we can step out of our overwhelming schedules and find clarity and rest in the presence of Jesus. You can read lots of organizational books, each filled with great tips, but this is one of the best I can offer. I have

found no greater source of focus and meaning than realigning my way-
ward thoughts with those of Jesus.

As we continue on through this book, you are going to read lots of
ideas for managing your life, time, office, and home. I pray this one sticks
with you when you feel overwhelmed. "I have told you these things, so that
in me you may have peace. In this world you will have trouble. But take
heart! I have overcome the world" (John 16:33).

Chapter Three

Increased Expectations

I started texting in earnest when we hired a twenty-one-year-old to help with our business. Our oldest child was sixteen and just starting to explore this expedited form of communication. Comparatively, Kortney was a near-professional. She could text with her eyes closed.

On the way to work one day, she texted me (not recommended) and asked if I wanted a coffee. I received her text and labored to respond. Before I could finish, she texted me again. It took a few tries to return to the previous screen, and again, before I could hit send, she texted me a third time.

Finally, I just gave up and called her. "Kortney," I said. "If you would stop texting me, I could respond!"

We laughed about that for weeks. Actually, I think she was laughing *at* me, but I enjoyed it, too.

Our culture has created a sense of urgency and expectation that's hard to shake. Whether it's a voice message, text, e-mail, instant message, or Facebook comment, there's an understanding . . . no, expectation . . . that I must respond. And I don't want to disappoint.

Honestly, it appeals to my need to be needed. Someone wants my opinion or my help. At the very least, they want to connect with me in some way. They want me to know how they feel or what they are doing that day. If they are willing to share their lives with me, my part is to respond. Promptly. With creativity. And a bit of humor, if you please. It's exhausting.

I use the example of texting to illustrate what seems to be a societal issue: people expect us to respond to their requests with increasing speed and efficiency.

The expectations of others seems to be a common issue among women who used to be organized. It seems impossible to balance everyone's needs. There are no firm lines between our private and public lives, and it's turning some of us into people-pleasing maniacs. Sadly, this is self-sabotaging behavior.

In the previous chapter, I addressed the issue of information overload and its clarity-sucking tendencies. In this chapter, we'll explore how responding incorrectly to the expectations of others can be just as damaging. As women seeking to follow the example of Jesus, we may find it challenging to determine when we are pleasing others to an unhealthy degree and when we are simply choosing to live sacrificially. We find the answer by looking deeper than our actions, to our hearts.

Unhealthy Response to Expectations

Many women will admit to being people-pleasers. This is often a deep-rooted issue, based in how accepted they felt as children. Did they have to earn their parents' approval? Was there conditional love? Many well-meaning parents raise approval-seeking children by training their children to look to *them* for answers and approval. It's easy to justify this approach as wise and protective parenting.

Sadly, children who desire a parent's approval before feeling confident simply transfer that need to others as they grow. You can see how such insecurity might lead to overcommitment.

My friend Karen admits to fighting her people-pleasing tendencies. She grew up in a difficult home setting, without much affirmation from her family, and she learned at an early age to "perform" for approval. In spite of her upbringing, her personality is open and giving, and she often extravagantly offers help. The help doesn't always come from a healthy place, and as a result, she overcommits herself with others.

From the outside, people-pleasers are a joy to be around. They are generous team players and always there to help. If you need something done right, they are your go-to folks. Yet on the inside, fear of rejection presses the pedal to the metal for people-pleasers. For them, the fear of making someone unhappy is worse than the prospect of being overwhelmed.

Karen explains, "Because I grew up in a home that was broken, school became everything to me. That was where I got affirmation and recognition. I learned to put people outside my home over people inside my home.

"Fast forward to being a mom with three kids, I tend to do the same thing. Someone outside my home needs me, and I put my family and my projects on the back burner. I'm so afraid they will not like me and think I'm not capable. But I've learned to tell myself, 'Every need is not my calling.' Someone is called to do it, but it's not always me."

Karen is facing her people-pleasing tendencies with the truth about her worth in God's eyes. God is tenderly healing the wounds Karen received as a child. As God strengthens her, she builds healthy boundaries and finds more peace and order in her life.

The Root of the Problem

Jesus identified a similar people-pleasing tendency in his own followers. They were torn between obligations to others and obedience to him. They wanted to follow Jesus, but on their conditions. Jesus challenged this line of thinking, and he called them to a new level of obedience, one that forced them to choose what was most important. Read some of the words of Jesus:

Then Jesus said to his disciples, "Whoever wants to be my disciple must deny themselves and take up their cross and follow me. For whoever wants to save their life will lose it, but whoever loses their life for me will find it." (Matt. 16:24–25)

Another disciple said to him, "Lord, first let me go and bury my father." But Jesus told him, "Follow me, and let the dead bury their own dead." (Matt. 8:21–22)

"Go, sell everything you have and give to the poor, and you will have treasure in heaven. Then come, follow me." (Mark 10:21)

Still another said, "I will follow you, Lord; but first let me go back and say goodbye to my family." Jesus replied, "No one who puts a hand to the plow and looks back is fit for service in the kingdom of God." (Luke 9:61–62)

When the demands of others threatened prompt obedience, Jesus called them back to center. He challenged them with the unspoken question he asks us: Who are you going to follow?

If we don't settle our hearts on the answer to this question, we end up with an overwhelmed and overcommitted life. Our lives operate like a carnival bumper car, racing crazily one direction, only to crash into an obstacle and wildly turn another direction.

To bring some simplicity and sanity back into our minds, schedules, and homes, we must address the root of the problem. It may take some time to think this through, but start here:

1. Who is the master in your life?
2. Who is defining your priorities?

My life took on clarity and direction when I declared Jesus Christ to be my leader. Now, please know that even though I spoke those words with my mouth, it took years to bring every area of my life into alignment. It is still a process, and at times I have to check my reality against my intent.

Those of us who have made this declaration are learning that following God's will (not the will of others) brings peace and focus despite our circumstances. Declaring Jesus as leader breaks our bondage to the approval of others. We can't follow and try to please two leaders without stress.

I love how the apostle Paul put it, "Obviously, I'm not trying to win the approval of people, but of God. If pleasing people were my goal, I would not be Christ's servant" (Gal. 1:10 NLT).

Exchanging a Maze for a Highway

Without a clear understanding of whom we are following, we'll wander in circles, and getting organized will be just a pretty pastime. God wants more than that for us.

God gave us two areas of life to manage: our time and our resources. We can't give ourselves even one minute of one day, and everything we own is a gift from God. Since it all came from God, it makes sense to care more about what he thinks than about what anyone else thinks. Otherwise, we are fractured, trying to please everyone, and searching for purpose.

Declaring whom you follow drives your life. It defines your purpose, establishes your goals, and gives you guidelines for how you spend your time and money.

In *The Purpose Driven Life*, Rick Warren says, "People who don't know their purpose try to do too much—and that causes stress, fatigue and conflict. It's impossible to do everything people want you to do. You have just enough time to do God's will. If you can't get it all done, it means you're trying to do more than God intended for you to do."[1]

If you've already made the declaration about whom you follow, it's a good time to consider whether your life reflects that decision. Do your priorities reflect that decision? We are going to talk about setting priorities in a later chapter, so let the question marinate for awhile.

For now, I'd like to address how to deal with the increased expectations of others in a practical way. Having a plan always helps me deal wisely when someone asks for my help. That plan includes when to say "yes" and when to say "no."

At Times, We Need to Say Yes

Addressing people-pleasing tendencies doesn't mean saying no to everyone. It means saying yes at the right time and no at other times.

There are some people who will always move to the top of my priority list.

- My husband
- My children
- My mother
- My sisters and their families ·
- My Proverbs 31 Ministries team members

Most times, I drop everything for them. But not always. If someone has a chronic tendency to wait until the last minute (aka, my children) and then holler for help, that's a different matter. It's like a youth pastor once said to his children, "A lack of planning on your part doesn't constitute an emergency on mine."

When my children ask for help, I determine if a "yes" would actually help them or hurt them. When my seventeen-year-old son asks me to make him a sandwich—and I'm sitting at my desk while he's watching television—the answer is no. He tried to tell me once that he doesn't know how to make a grilled cheese sandwich. He got a cooking lesson that day.

However, when my husband asks for my help, it goes to the top of my to-do list. Whether it's making an appointment for an oil change or calling the accountant, if I can help lighten his load, I'll do it. I've learned to ask him for a deadline. That way I've eliminated assumptions on both our parts and can work it into my schedule.

These core relationships ground my life. These people come before anyone or anything else. Even though they are at the top of my priority list, and they are going to get a "yes" whenever possible, there are still ways to schedule my response and meet both our needs.

For everyone else in my life, taking time before answering is the best approach. There is wisdom in weighing a new request against current and future commitments. With time to think, the answer is often an obvious "no." The next problem is how to communicate that response.

How to Say No

But I don't want to hurt her feelings!

Most of us never want to hurt another's feelings. Even if we don't have people-pleasing problems, we can still be overcommitted because we can't say no. Learning to say no will give you the freedom to make choices about your time and free you up to attend to your own responsibilities. That's why it's time to learn how to say no with grace and kindness.

The truth is always the best approach when saying no. Keep it simple. People don't need to hear your sob story. A five-minute exposition about your busy life, your demanding mother, or your clinging children isn't the most effective approach. That may be the truth, but you've given too much information, and your listener tuned out four minutes ago.

Since I'm a get-it-done kind of gal, people frequently ask me for help. Requests come from leaders at church, my children's school, neighbors, and friends. Then there are important jobs that need to be done on my children's sports teams or for Girl Scouts. Every request for my help has value. It's all worthwhile. But it's not all mine to do.

Ask for Time to Decide

When someone asks for your help, ask for time to pray about it. If you don't feel comfortable saying "pray," then ask for time to "think." Then take it to God. By establishing this pattern, you've built in a response time and eliminated a response based on emotion such as guilt or sympathy.

God may surprise you with his answer. It may be yes. It may be no. Either way, you are learning to seek God's approval rather than that of other people, and that is the first step to a healthy schedule. Here's how to say it:

I'd like to pray/think about that. When do you need an answer?
I need to check my schedule. I'll get back to you in a few days.

Ask for More Information

Get a complete picture of the task. Ask how much time it will take and what's involved. You might also ask to speak with someone who has done it before. It's called due diligence, and in doing it, you may discover a conflict that makes it easy to say no.

I'd like to know more. Can you write up a description of
what's involved?
That sounds interesting, but I'd like to get an accurate picture of
what would be required of me before I decide.

Scripts for Saying No

If you don't believe this request fits into your life at this time, then decline with a simple answer that doesn't invite questions. Normally, I express my appreciation and honor for being asked, and then I offer a response such as:

God is calling me to simplify my schedule. As much as I would love
to help, I need to say no.
I'm trying to be a better steward of my time. As important as this
request is, I hope you understand, but I need to decline.
I'm trying to focus on my main priorities and need to say no at
this time.

These are confident responses that show you've thought this out. Most people respect these types of answers and respect you for giving them. Do not open the door for a "yes" later on. It only postpones the inevitable and increases your stress.

There are other requests that take time away from my priorities. Here are two common issues, with my response scripts.

E-mail forwards. Reading funny stories is amusing, but they are mind clutter when I'm trying to accomplish a task.

> *I love getting your forwards, but I'm trying to simplify my inbox. Do you mind taking me off your forward list?*

Requests for help with technology. You might have people in your life who refuse to learn how to program the DVD player, pay a bill online, or print out directions from MapQuest. Why should they learn if they have you?

> *Can I show you how to do that, so you can do it next time?*

Renewed Focus

As you establish a plan for responding to requests and set boundaries around your time, you'll discover a renewed focus for your day. It's a sense of freedom, really. You've been bound to the expectations of others, and you no longer are. You are free to set your own priorities and manage your life accordingly. It's not the answer to an organized life, but it's a good foundation.

Section Two

finding a Balanced Approach to an Ordered Life

Chapter Four

I'm Somewhere in Here

Everyone wants to find balance. We imagine there's a perfect formula to manage the many demands on our lives with graceful flair. Yet something's often out of whack. From experience, I can say that the more I try to control the world around me, the more out of balance life gets. That's because focusing more on the outside than the inside results in a house of cards.

For years I did just that. When an unexpected move shook the foundations of everything I knew, the dangers of building my life on accomplishments became a painful reality. That's why I had to include this chapter. If every inch of your home is in order and your schedule mastered, but your heart is empty, I would have done you a disservice with this book.

So for the next few chapters, I want to share my story of how God challenged me to match my outsides with my insides. I had to reevaluate my priorities and my expectations for myself. It was a time of brutal honesty, loneliness, and shattered pride. But it was drenched in a message of hope and redemption.

In the middle of it all, I learned a truth about myself that reshaped my future. Three little words helped me find myself under all the mess and discover the woman God created me to be. May they do the same for you.

I Was Born to Do This . . . Wasn't I?

I was born to be a professional woman. As least that's what I always thought. Perhaps growing up at the height of the women's lib movement grounded that belief. It certainly wasn't my role model at home. My mom stayed home with my little sister and me, always had dinner on the table at 5:30 p.m., and ironed my dad's handkerchiefs. She supported me unconditionally, but she never pushed me toward either homemaking or professional work.

The reasons behind my assumptions aren't important, just know they were unshakable. College and a career were my goals, and a family on the side would be nice, thank you very much. While other little girls played house and dreamed of having children, I organized clubs and made myself president. My Barbie was CEO, while Ken looked good.

The Early Years

My husband Tod and I met and married in college. He's always been supportive of my goals, so he was fully on board. We both wanted children in five years and figured we'd add them to our lives and proceed as planned.

At the end of our five-year plan, we started trying to have a family. Within a few months, we learned getting pregnant isn't as easy as flipping an "on" switch. In hindsight, this was a foreshadowing of how little control we would actually have in coming years.

One year passed, and doctors stamped "infertility" on my charts. Year two passed with lots of tests, tears, and thoughts of adoption filling the days. Year three was almost past when in the not-so-romantic setting of a doctor's office, our first son became more than a dream.

Joshua Owen Whitwer changed the world as I knew it . . . forever. Interestingly, I didn't accept the changes. I adored my little son and loved him more than I thought possible. But I never considered changing my life plans for him. After a short maternity break, I returned to work.

Apparently, the infertility issues were in the past, because twenty-six months later, Dylan was born, and twenty-one months after that, Robbie joined the family. Then we had to figure out how to stop this runaway train.

The next three years were the hardest of my life. Frustration reigned in my heart and mind as I tried to regain my "old" life. It was like trying to walk against the current . . . in mud up to my knees . . . carrying three children in my arms. Let's just say it wasn't graceful. But I'll tell you more about that in a later chapter. For now, I want you to get a picture of the woman I was: administratively inclined, a leader, in control, and involved with everything.

Although every day was a struggle, I envisioned life returning to normal when Robbie started school. In spite of the frustration, it was a good life. The boys were healthy, Tod had a good job, my position allowed me to work part time, I was active in church, I sang in the choir, and I led children's and parts of women's ministries. My parents and two of my sisters lived close by, and we had a snug little house with a fenced pool in the backyard.

Don't Get Too Comfortable

On a warm April day, Tod announced his company was closing their Phoenix office. He was the manager and had only been with them ten months. They offered him a job in Denver, but we weren't interested in moving.

Tod had a few months to close up the office and find a new position. We weren't really worried because, being a consultant, Tod had many professional connections in Phoenix. I was completely unprepared for happened next.

Within a week after the closure announcement, Tod received a call from a friend who had moved to North Carolina. This friend had a job he wanted Tod to consider. We still had no plans to move, but Tod wanted to check it out. So he flew to Charlotte, all the while saying, "I'm not interested, I just want to see what he has to say."

Can you guess what happened next? After a job offer, stormy conversations, and lots of tears, we packed up, rented our house, and moved to the South. An important part of this story is that my husband wanted to move back to Phoenix in two or three years.

That makes it sound much neater than it really was. Let me back up and give you a longer and more accurate version. The truth is, I was a bitter, angry, and resentful woman. The injustice of the situation consumed me. I was convinced moving was not in God's will for me, and I told my husband so. With one hand on my hip and another sharply pointed at him, I snapped, "Just because your name rhymes with God doesn't mean you know his will!" Yep, it wasn't pretty.

In spite of my anger, a feather-like thought tickled inside. I knew Tod had never demanded his way in the past, and in fact, he wasn't demanding it then either. If I said no, then we wouldn't move. But I also knew that if I said no, I would be squelching a dream he'd had for many years, which was to live in a different city. And next time, it could be a less desirable destination.

In a moment of teeth-gritting determination, I said yes and committed not to complain, and we moved. But in my heart, I was a mess. I'm ashamed to say that I believed my husband had stepped so far out of God's plan that I was destined to suffer for two years. While outwardly submissive, inwardly my heart was darkly rebellious. I decided to make the best of it, get through the next two years, return to Arizona, and pick up where I had left off.

Even though my husband only wanted to move for a few years, it made no difference. I continually asked myself, "How could he be so selfish? How could he ask me to move across the country and leave everything I love—my work, my ministry, my family?"

About that commitment not to complain—I was actually successful. But I sure did mope a lot. Poison and bitterness filled my thought life.

Could It Get Any Worse?

Everything about the South was beautiful except my heart. Even there, the décor was changing. The anger that sustained me during the move left shortly after we arrived, and low self-esteem and depression blindsided me. I felt like a nobody.

I never thought I had a self-esteem problem until no one knew my talents: that I could sing, write, and successfully organize a special event. All my accomplishments and achievements meant nothing to anyone.

When every accomplishment was stripped away, what was left was an unhappy, self-centered woman who didn't think God could make anything good out of a miserable situation. Instead of seeing what I had, I focused on what I didn't have.

When I wasn't crying, I was trying to make some kind of a home to live in. At a local Christian bookstore, I found a book called *No Ordinary Home* by an author named Carol Brazo. It was subtitled *The Uncommon Art of Christ-Centered Homemaking*. Since I was going to be a full-time homemaker for the next two years, I decided to figure out what it meant. Hey, here was another accomplishment I could master.

What I learned from reading the book was more than dusting techniques or time management tools. I learned a life-changing truth about how God sees me and how I should see myself. She says:

> If there were one biblical truth I wish I could give my children and lay hold of in my own deepest parts, it would be this one thing. He created me, He loves me, He will always love me. Nothing I do will change who I am.
>
> Being versus doing. The error was finally outlined in bold. I was always worried about what I was doing.
>
> God's only concerns was and is what I am being—a child of His, forgiven, justified by the work of His Son, His heir.
>
> He did everything that needed doing; I need to relax and concentrate on being. The only thing I need to do is come to grips with God's way of seeing me.[1]

Being versus Doing

Those simple words pierced my heart. The book dropped in my lap as tears filled my eyes. She was talking about me.

When the last tissue was shredded, a new creation rose from the couch. *Being* versus *doing*—those three words redefined my understanding of what God wanted of me. It was as if God took a key, turned the lock, and removed the heavy chains of expectation I'd used to shackle myself.

That was just the start of the transformation God had planned for me. Shortly, through a series of events only he could orchestrate, God connected me with Proverbs 31 Ministries. Probably not a coincidence that God connected me with a Christian women's organization based in Charlotte, with the calling "Touching Women's Hearts, Building Godly Homes." My heart needed more than touching at that time. It needed a good swat.

As I became involved in this ministry, God revealed that my view of my life and purpose was small compared to his. I had separated all the areas of my life and was destroying myself trying to keep everything balanced. Not only was I suffering, but I shortchanged everyone I loved, including God. It was as if my priorities were upside down.

As the truth of my identity in Christ became a reality in my life, I realized I was not the person God wanted me to be. The selfishness the move revealed had been there all along. Even though my life looked good on the outside, the truth is that self-interest motivated much of my life. Did my husband meet my needs? Did my children meet my needs? Did my church meet my needs? Did my job meet my needs? Me, me, me.

God pulled me out of the workplace and away from everything I loved to show me that it wasn't all about me. It was and is all about Jesus and how my heart reflected him.

To-Do Lists Will Never Satisfy

By now, you must be wondering how this chapter fits in with a book on reclaiming organizational skills. It fits because disappointment always follows pursuing significance and identity in accomplishments. Productive women like you and me will always struggle with keeping our priorities right. It's much easier to focus on what we can check off our to-do list.

Yet without a deep understanding that our significance comes from being loved and accepted by God exactly as we are, upside-down priorities will dominate our lives. We will be like addicts looking for that next project to feel good about ourselves. We will overload our schedules, overcommit our resources, and leave a path of regrets.

There has to be a certain amount of frustration in your life that prompted you to read this book. I know. I've been there. You probably feel that some of your life is out of control, and if you could only get through those stacks on your kitchen counter, you'd feel better about life in general. Yet the truth is, you can have the most organized garage on the block, but if your insides don't match your outsides, you'll always be out of alignment.

Time for a Self-Evaluation

Years ago, I rarely examined my heart condition. I never checked myself for judgmental thoughts, critical words, or selfish motives. I didn't address fear as a lack of faith—I just avoided certain issues. My love for God was strong, but deep within I was motivated to prove myself worthy by what I did. That's a dangerous place to land.

The Bible is clear that God places more value on my heart than my achievements. Jesus was passionate about having a heart that was pure. He reserved his harshest criticism for those who looked good on the outside but were spiritually dead on the inside. The Old Testament tells the story of King David, a man whose heart was in the right place although his actions weren't flawless. There's a great story in 1 Samuel 16 about when the prophet Samuel met David for the first time.

God directed Samuel to Bethlehem to find King Saul's replacement among the sons of Jesse. God didn't say which son, just that he would anoint the chosen one.

Saul went to Bethlehem, invited Jesse and his sons to a sacrifice, and waited. As Jesse and sons arrived, Saul's eyes traveled to Eliab, the eldest son. I imagine Eliab was the tallest, strongest, and most self-assured. Saul thought, "Surely the Lord's anointed stands here."

But God surprised Saul and said, "Do not consider his appearance or his height, for I have rejected him. The Lord does not look at the things man looks at. Man looks at the outward appearance, but the Lord looks at the heart." God proceeded to anoint David, the youngest, who wasn't even considered a candidate by his earthly father.

While I want you to regain control over your home, office, and schedule, I want even more for you to be centered in God's will. I believe if your heart is where God wants it to be, you'll see things with new eyes, have more peace, and feel less pressure to get things just so.

Before moving on, take some time for a self-examination. Are there things in your heart that need some attention? Some red flags might include:

- Comparing yourself to others.
- Being overly concerned with what others think or say.
- Putting tasks over people.
- Entertaining resentful, unkind thoughts about others.
- Unforgiveness.
- Believing that you're the only one who can get things done.
- Judgmental thoughts.

If you do find wrong thoughts and attitudes have taken root in your heart, confess those to God. Then confess them to someone you trust. In my experience, as I confess my weak and sinful heart issues, God starts to bring healing through his Word or through wise counsel.

To find our way to a place of healthy balance, we'll need to address these issues one way or another. Hopefully you can do this before God does something drastic like he did with me. Although, even if that happens, it will be good.

Chapter Five

Setting Reasonable Expectations for Yourself

Of you just finished Chapter Four, you know my husband and I met in college, married while still students, and had a great plan for our lives. In the last chapter, I skipped a few years between Robbie's birth and our move to Charlotte. What happened during those years helped set the stage for God's work in my life. I'd like to go back and give you an insider's view of how I got to that place of bitterness before the move.

Before I do that, I want to point out that earlier in the book I mentioned being a mother of five. Our two daughters joined our family in 2005 from war-torn Liberia, Africa. I could write another book about all God has done in our lives through those precious girls. But for this story, most of what I learned happened before God established us as a family of seven.

When Robbie was born, Josh was still three years old. And they were all active boys! It was really quite an eye-opening experience for me. My father was a teacher who listened to classical music, and my mother was a book lover, seamstress, and church secretary. To say I had a quiet, sedentary childhood was an understatement.

My husband and I were outnumbered, and my life was completely upended. For the next three years, I couldn't even go shopping at Target by myself with the boys. While Josh raced down the aisle, Dylan climbed out of the cart—all while Robbie, who disliked being confined from the moment of his birth, screamed. I was a mess! I felt like climbing over the cart and racing down the aisle screaming, too.

When I should have been enjoying the happy chaos and accepting my life as it was, I kept trying to regain my old life and slammed into daily frustration. My normally clean house was in constant clutter. Balls, toys, sippy cups, and blankies littered couches, beds, and every floor in the house. In addition to the disorganization, we couldn't seem to catch up on repair projects. We lived with a half-painted family room, featuring a hole in the wall (a result of some overzealous play) for years.

An organizer and leader by nature, I'd volunteer to oversee something at church and then make my kids and me miserable trying to get it done. My heart is heavy when I remember the times I dragged my three little boys to one event or another, only to leave angry and in tears because they couldn't sit still.

Instead of accepting my life as it was and thriving where I was, I plowed ahead, wanting to serve God and certain he was pleased with my sacrifices. The problem was that my innocent children and husband made the real sacrifices by enduring my nonstop lifestyle. I wish with all my heart that someone had taken me out to coffee and helped me get some perspective.

Priorities Change When Life Changes

God gave me three new priorities in little blue blankets. While I wanted to disrupt my life as little as possible with the changes, God wanted an overhaul.

Caring for those three boys changed almost everything about me— starting with my clothing and shoe sizes. For about three years, I didn't get enough sleep. I was working outside the home and had very little spare time. The noise level in my house made it hard for me to think, and my energy level was at an all-time low.

And yet I still held myself to the same standards of organization that I managed to adhere to before I had children. I felt like a failure at everything. If I were honest, I also felt fear. I saw my life changes as hurdles to overcome. As quickly as possible. So that I didn't miss out. That attitude kept me from embracing my current situation and learning new techniques to thrive where I was.

There may be nothing you can change about your situation, but you can change your expectations. In this chapter, we'll look at responding to changes in a healthy way. Becoming a woman who sets healthy expectations for herself based on reality will bring a greater sense of acceptance, peace, and hope to your life. With this attitude, you'll tune in to what God is doing and be open to new opportunities.

In addition to setting healthy expectations for ourselves, we also need to nurture our faith and physical health.

You can delegate responsibility for many areas of your life. You can hire cleaning help, eat out every night, or ask a friend to run errands. But you can't delegate responsibility for your faith or your health.

Accept and Thrive

My normal changed for joyous reasons. Some women's normal changes for employment reasons, a move, or a big event—like a wedding. Yet others face changes for more difficult reasons: the declining health of ourselves or a loved one, grief, loss of employment, or someone else's unplanned need. No matter what we face today, we can grow and thrive.

As surprised and overwhelmed by our current condition as we might be, nothing surprises our Heavenly Father. He is not wringing his hands in heaven wondering how you are going to get help. He already has a plan for your rescue.

Please realize, this doesn't always mean changing our situations. But it always means changing us. God uses every challenge we face to bring us good. Don't forget, God's definition of "good" is often different than ours. Good doesn't always mean he'll help us get our houses organized or our babies eating and sleeping on schedule. While that may seem good to us now, God is concerned with more than momentary convenience.

While God doesn't always remove the difficult circumstances, he's always doing something. God's good in my life in the midst of tough times is usually revealed afterward. In hindsight, I came to a more intimate knowledge of God's character, developed greater compassion for others, and reached a deeper level of dependence and faith. In times of fear, God has shown his power by bringing peace.

Today you may feel overwhelmed by circumstances you didn't see on the horizon. Jesus spoke these encouraging words recorded in John 16:33:

> "I have told you these things, so that in me you may have peace. In this world you will have trouble. But take heart! I have overcome the world."

By steadfastly believing God is doing something good, you will find meaning in your difficult changes. There aren't always answers to "Why, God?" Instead, try asking, "What do you want me to learn?" "How do you want me to change?" Lean into changes rather than pulling away. In time, you'll see the fullness of God's good plan for you.

Guard Your Spiritual Health

Staying connected with God is crucial to finding balance and perspective during challenging times. There are no rules for this, despite what you may have heard. Some people call it "quiet time," but if kids are playing loudly, it may be far from quiet. Find what works best for you, and don't worry about what the "experts" say. Here are some suggestions:

- Schedule a "staff meeting" with God. If you are a businessperson, you might enjoy taking a more professional approach. Take time to listen to your boss, share your concerns, and take good notes.

- Write your personal to-do list before praying or your "quiet" time. It will help clear your mind.
- Pray when you can. Pray when doing laundry, driving, or waiting in the carpool lane.
- Download free podcasts of great pastors to your iPod. My favorites are Andy Stanley and Rob Bell.
- Carry inspirational material with you. Get a devotional app or Bible for your phone, or carry a bag with a small Bible or devotional book. Pull it out when waiting for an appointment.
- Don't compare yourself to anyone in this regard. Like any parent, God is delighted when you seek him out—whatever that looks like.

Take Care of Yourself

If you are struggling to regain a sense of control over your life, consider whether your health has been compromised in some way. This can happen due to age or stressful situations. If you are experiencing chronic exhaustion or the "blues" that don't improve, there may be an underlying health issue. Although this book will help with some practical changes, you may want to address the physical part of your life with professional support.

My younger sister recently addressed this issue in her own life. She was struggling at work with staying focused and keeping up. Financial cutbacks didn't help as her department budget dropped and her boss added responsibilities. After a few family mini-traumas occurred in rapid succession, my normally composed and efficient sister was at a breaking point. She went to her doctor and within minutes was diagnosed with ADD. She decided to take medicine and now has a renewed vigor and hope.

After eliminating hidden physical issues as the problem, it's time to develop a fresh and healthy approach to organization. First, addressing self-expectations is critical. We might need to tell our bossy old self to take it easy on our overwhelmed new self. Self-care and compassion create a safe nest to develop new wings.

Set Aside Time to Think

Time to think is precious to an overwhelmed woman. My first instinct when my to-do list is longer than Rapunzel's hair is to start doing something . . . anything. I'm driven by a sense of urgency to check items off that list. Once I make that first move, I'm a goner.

Thinking releases me from the chains of the urgent to a higher level of planning. Instead of examining issues with a magnifying glass, I've got a strategic viewpoint with less emotion and more objectivity. Do you find it hard to carve out thinking time? Here are some suggestions for cultivating quiet:

- Value thinking time. What we value, we find time to do.
- Turn off the TV. Instead of watching the morning news, grab a cup of coffee and just think.
- Turn off the radio in the car.
- Walk with no iPod.

Things to Think About

- Five things you are thankful for.
- What you would like to change about yourself.
- How you would like to improve your home or time management.
- New ways to address a problem.
- Ideas for showing love to those closest to you.
- Your dreams.
- Your priorities.
- Your inner motivations for your emotional responses.
- Why you will be a better person if you forgive someone.

Watch What You Eat

In times of transition and stress, healthy eating takes second place to the urgent needs put before us. Yet, a healthy diet can increase energy and mental focus. I address part of this issue in Chapter Sixteen on meal planning. Yet it bears repeating here.

When my first child was born, I was clueless. Josh weighed nine pounds and two ounces and was ready for a Big Mac at about two months. During the first two weeks, Josh and I got into a downward spiral: he cried and then I cried. We just took turns crying.

I was trying to nurse him, but he was always hungry. I just bounced him in my arms for hours. Nothing helped. Sadly, no one told me I needed to drink and eat in order to make milk for him. And in the stress of a constantly crying baby, I barely ate. A friend made me a loaf of bread and peach preserves, and that was breakfast and lunch for the first week. It wasn't enough. I should have cared for myself first.

Make sure your diet consists of the following things.

Multivitamins. Ideally, your diet should fulfill all of your vitamin and mineral needs. If a lack of energy is part of the problem, consider multivitamins for a time. Don't scrimp on quality. Dollar store brands don't easily dissolve and can pass right through your body.

Water. Consider water as fuel for your cells. Dehydration can happen quickly, so try to drink your six to eight glasses of water a day. Do whatever you need to do to make drinking water more enjoyable.

- Buy bendy straws.
- Use a special glass.
- Have fun with ice cube trays in the shape of hearts.

Fruits and vegetables. Although smoothies and juices are tasty and easy to consume, whole fruits and vegetables are a healthier choice due to increased fiber.

- Wash grapes and cut into easy-to-grab sections.
- Wash and cut fresh fruit in the morning. Take it with you to work in resealable baggies, or set it on the counter at home.
- Slice cucumbers for a fresh snack.
- Store cut broccoli and cauliflower florets for easy snacking or salad toppings.

Top Ten Fruits

1. Avocado	6. Apricots (dried, unsulfured)
2. Papaya	7. Mango
3. Guava	8. Strawberries (organic)
4. Cantaloupe	9. Kiwi
5. Orange	10. Grapefruit (pink or red)

(According to www.AskDrSears.com and based on vitamin C, fiber, carotenoids, calcium, and folic acid.)

Complex carbohydrates. Sneak these in whenever possible.

- Use multi-grain and whole wheat products when possible: pasta, breads, pancake mixes.
- Cook with more beans: bean soup, ham and beans, or just top your salad with them.

The other good stuff. Consume less caffeine, leaner meats, more fish, healthy oil, more antioxidant-rich food. Most of us know this—we just don't always incorporate these items into our diet.

Rest

When my children were babies, I understood the power of sleep deprivation as torture. I couldn't think straight and wasn't rational. Getting enough sleep is critical for mental clarity and energy to organize. Here are my best tips for proper sleep if this is a problem for you. If it's not a problem, then read on.

- Be honest about how much you need. Five hours isn't enough for most people. I need about seven or eight.
- Read the Bible before going to sleep. God's peace rests on me after reading his Word.
- Limit evening activities and have a wind-down period.
- No naps (unless you have a newborn). Otherwise, you will start a cycle of needing to nap and not sleeping enough at night.

You Will Not Be Forgotten

What I know now is that sometimes God calls us to a new mission field that on the surface looks as if we've been called out of the "game." But nothing could be further from the truth! During my early child-raising years, I was afraid to stop pursuing my goals in case an opportunity might pass me by. I was worried and anxious because I couldn't get my old life back.

Not only was that a fantasy, but in my striving, the opportunity to minister more deeply to my children and husband passed me by.

Second Peter 3:8 says, "But do not forget this one thing, dear friends: With the Lord a day is like a thousand years, and a thousand years are like a day." Although this verse is speaking about the Lord's return, I believe we can apply it to any time of "waiting." God doesn't see time as we do. Three years seems like an eternity, when it's really just a breath in time. The first part of verse nine offers hope to those who think opportunities are passing them by and God has forgotten them: "The Lord is not slow in keeping his promise, as some understand slowness."

I wish someone had told me that God would not forget me, that I was right where he wanted me and that I should relax, accept my new normal, and see the opportunities he had placed in front of me. Even though my days felt like years, they really were just a blink. At least, that's what I know now. . . .

The same is true for you. Life has changed. Demands have changed. You have changed. God hasn't. His promise and vision for you is intact. Rest in that truth.

Chapter Six

Establishing Priorities

By nine this morning I was already overwhelmed. Deadlines loomed, laundry piled, and my to-do list screamed. Two responses battled for dominance: 1) just start doing something on my task list . . . preferably something easy; or 2) do something completely different, like play solitaire. My instinct in that moment of indecision was anything but wise. My initial leaning when overwhelmed is usually to start working on something, anything, instead of taking a moment and focusing on my priorities for that day.

This reaction-based approach hinders my ability to organize my thoughts, tasks, home, and office. I become a micromanager, avoiding the big picture while focused on the details. Instead of bringing focus to my work, I shift and shuffle the urgent, important, and interesting tasks before me.

It's a daily battle. Each day, my approach depends on a variety of elements:

- My energy level.
- My available time.
- The most urgent deadline.

- My interest level in the task.
- The number of unimportant but interesting e-mails in my inbox.

Thankfully, underneath those surface-level factors, a deeper river of motivation runs: my priorities. It's how I stepped back this morning from panic-driven decision making to a place of simple, calm focus. Does it always happen? No. Sometimes I jump into the fray with both feet. Usually those days end with me shrugging my shoulders and wondering why nothing got done. It's like going to the grocery store, spending a hundred dollars, and having nothing for dinner.

I learned long ago that planning my day based on priorities rather than urgency gives me a much greater sense of peace and purpose. My days can still fall apart and deteriorate into fighting fires, but those days are less frequent.

Establishing priorities for my life helps me combat the instinct to immerse myself in busy work. Busy work is easy, and there's great satisfaction in checking items off a to-do list. Yet it's scary to see how quickly mundane work can fill our days. Then we find ourselves looking over the past, wondering where the time went.

Weeks, months, and years fly by, and regret often nags the edges of our conscience. "If onlys" sprinkle conversation. How many people wish they had finished college, visited their Grandma one more time, or written that book? We want to have a purpose-filled life, but somehow it just seems too difficult to take time to establish priorities, set goals, and then make the hard choices. When we don't set and live by priorities, we establish patterns of regret.

Years ago, I heard author Kevin Lehman make this observation at a conference: "You can either choose the pain of discipline now, or the pain of regret later. Regret lasts longer."

In this chapter, I want to help you stop the busy work for a moment and focus on God's priorities for you. Regret isn't mandatory. I believe you can live life with purpose and contentment, and it starts with understanding God's will for your life. But can the average person know God's will?

How Can I Know God's Will for My Life?

Some think it's presumptuous to believe we can know God's will. Yet the Bible makes it clear God isn't withholding that information. Romans 12:2 says, "Do not conform to the pattern of this world, but be transformed by the renewing of your mind. Then you will be able to test and approve what God's will is—his good, pleasing and perfect will."

According to these words by the apostle Paul, we can know God's will and his priorities for us. This verse gives two conditions for knowing God's will:

- Not conforming to the pattern of the world.
- Being transformed by the renewing of our minds.

The pattern of this world will obscure God's priorities for us every time, because it creates a self-centered life. A self-centered life is one in which we consistently choose what the Bible calls the "ways of this world." That typically means following our own desires, regardless of whether they line up with God's ways. Ephesians 2:1–3a explains in greater detail:

> As for you, you were dead in your transgressions and sins, in which you used to live when you followed the ways of this world and of the ruler of the kingdom of the air, the spirit who is now at work in those who are disobedient. All of us also lived among them at one time, gratifying the cravings of our flesh and following its desires and thoughts.

We live among parallel kingdoms constantly at war: the kingdom of God and that of Satan. Scripture tells us that Satan is the "ruler of the kingdom of the air," the "prince of this world" (John 14:30). However, Jesus ushered in God's kingdom—hence the conflict.

A spiritual battle storms around us at all times. It's not for land or money—but for our hearts. When we weave between the two kingdoms—choosing between the ways of the world and God's ways—our hearts are divided. A divided heart always faces confusion.

In hindsight, my own life reflects this conflict. Even as a committed Christian, I didn't understand the need to seek God's will above my own. For years, I pursued priorities that took me further spiritually from where God wanted me. It was as if I let God in my car, but only into the backseat. My inner struggle resulted in frustration and annoyance, which often spilled out onto those I loved.

Beware of Looking Good

Outsiders might have looked at my priorities years ago and nodded in affirmation. They "looked" good. My resume included pursuing a demanding career in public relations, serving on nonprofit boards, leading ministries at church, singing on the praise team, and spearheading any exciting project presented at work or church. It was a full and productive life. Just not the one God had in mind for me.

The Bible is very clear that some choices may seem wise at first glance, but the foundations are shaky. Just like walking along a boardwalk with rotten wood—you may not realize its weakness until you are in the water looking up. Colossians 2:8 says, "See to it that no one takes you captive through hollow and deceptive philosophy, which depends on human tradition and the elemental spiritual forces of this world rather than on Christ."

If you read my story in Chapter Four, you'll know what God did to get my attention. Before that, I wasn't seeking to pattern my life after Christ. My personal choices were based on my desire for advancing my goals rather than his. From the outside, it might be a subtle difference; on the inside, it was a revolution.

Not only did that move to Charlotte transform my heart, but it reordered my priorities. My personal reordering started with redefining my primary place of ministry from church to home. That was a paradigm shift for me, which launched the upheaval of every other priority in my life. It also led me into the second part of knowing God's will: transforming my mind.

Renew Your Mind

My mind was stuck on me—my career, my plans, my needs. Apparently I needed an earthquake to get unstuck. Once that shift happened, it didn't take long to see truth—about myself and my life. God sweetly began the process of renewing my mind, which continues to this day.

Every day I have a choice to make: God's priorities or mine? When it's a good day, and I make a choice to seek God's priorities before my own, a mental adjustment, a renewing happens and clarity follows. Like a dancer who focuses on one point while twirling—I maintain balance no matter what swirls around me. You see, I can have a house that looks great, all my files in place, and never forget an appointment, but that doesn't ensure a balanced, solid life.

That's why these chapters are placed before any of those offering tips and strategies for reclaiming your organization skills. Without a deeper exploration of God's priorities for you, you'll just juggle your existing commitments and end up even more frustrated.

Define Your Priorities

The questions now turn to you. Are you clear on your priorities? If so, does your schedule reflect them? Maybe I should ask you to review your calendar first. Your schedule (and checkbook) always reveals the truth about priorities. If your schedule is unmanageable and overwhelming, it's likely your priorities are in the wrong place.

There is an exception to that statement. Sometimes situations collide, and for a time our schedules are crazy. People get sick, co-workers quit, or finances are tight. Situational craziness isn't the issue. It's long-term unmanageability.

If you've been living with upside down priorities for long, you probably live with an underlying sense of regret and frustration. You know that nagging feeling you can't identify? Without a healthy grid for making time decisions, you will say yes to more than you can handle, or to the wrong things.

God has given each of us enough time, energy, finances, and resources to accomplish what he wants us to accomplish. That is amazing to me. I am already equipped for what I'm supposed to do. Sadly, I've wasted time in the past trying to do things God called others to do. And I've held on to responsibilities longer than I should.

When that happens, my life is out of balance. The things I value most get the least amount of my time and often the lowest amount of energy and enthusiasm. It's a constant challenge to bring life back into a healthy balance. I start by asking myself a series of questions that bring me back to center.

Questions to Define Priorities

One way I evaluate whether I'm living according to God's priorities is to work through a set of questions. By taking the time to process these questions, I press the pause button for a few moments. By doing so, I reposition myself from the center of the busyness to a peaceful place outside the fray.

I also ask God for wisdom and confirmation as I consider these important questions. I don't want to race ahead if they aren't God's priorities. Writing the answers down can bring clarity to my thinking and give me a touchstone for the future. Following are the five questions I ask.

What can only I do?

There are some jobs in my life no one else can do. If I had the money, I could hire someone to clean my house and do my laundry. Someone else could edit the *P31 Woman* magazine. Someone else could teach the writing class I teach. However, no one else can nurture my personal faith in God. Only I can do that. No one else can get my body to the gym or limit my sugar intake. I have the final decision on those responsibilities.

The same applies to my marriage and children. I am the only woman who is Tod's wife. Unless I want to abdicate that role, it is up to me to become the best wife I can be. And God has given me five children to mother. Those four areas of life (plus a few others) are no-brainers to me, and they will always be at the top of my priority list.

What has God entrusted to me?

Everyone has responsibility for some resources. We all have a certain amount of money, a home, talents, and intelligence. God also entrusts us with the care of others—children are obvious, but sometimes we care for parents or grandparents. God has given some of us opportunities. What has God entrusted to you?

Am I a good steward of what I already have?

This is where I do a painful assessment of reality. How am I doing with what God has already given me? Are my finances a wreck? Have I neglected my husband? Have I honored my parents? God is always watching to see how I'm doing with what he's already given me. When he sees I manage things well, he entrusts me with more. When I'm neglectful, the opposite happens.

Jesus told a story in the Bible about a boss who gave three servants some money. Two invested the money and presented the boss with the original amount plus interest. One, however, hid his money in fear. The boss was unhappy with the one, but he was pleased with the other two. Here's what the boss said to the two, "Well done, good and faithful servant! You have been faithful with a few things; I will put you in charge of many things. Come and share your master's happiness!" (Matt. 25:23).

The story represents God's attitude toward us when we manage our responsibilities with excellence. Before he gives us more, he watches to see if he can trust us.

What passion (or dream) has God put in my heart?

Years ago, I watched a DVD series by Bruce Wilkinson based on his book *The Dream Giver*. As he spoke about the dreams God places in our hearts, my eyes filled with tears. I was embarrassed to be crying until I looked at my friends in the room. No one's eyes were dry. The dream God put in my heart was tender and vulnerable—it was to write a book. To even speak of it made my heart beat faster. This was no fleeting idea that sounded good. It wasn't a passing thought: *One day I ought to write a book*. I felt that "burning" in my chest when I thought of it. I knew it was from God.

I've felt that passion at other times as well. I felt it when I knew we were to adopt two little girls from Africa, I felt it serving on the worship team, and I feel it now about several projects I'm developing at Proverbs 31 Ministries. It's a different emotional response than how I feel about our next vacation or Christmas. It comes from a deeper place in my heart.

What passion or dream has God placed in your heart?

What has God asked me to do that I haven't done yet?

At the end of a Sunday service, around the time I was watching *The Dream Giver* DVDs, my pastor did an altar call of sorts. He said, "God has asked some of you to do something, and you haven't done it yet. If that's you, I want you to come up for prayer."

My heart wasn't beating just a bit faster. It was pounding. I knew that invitation was for me. God had asked me to write a book, and I kept putting it off. There was one excuse and fear after another. That day, I fled to the front of the room and confessed my disobedience. After that, writing a book shot way up on my priority list. Within a year of that altar call, I had a book contract.

I once heard this statement, "Old orders are standing orders." Meaning, if God asked you to do something years ago, and didn't revise the directions, he still expects you to do it. It's never too late to be obedient.

What Are My Priorities?	
What can only I do?	Develop my faith Take care of my health Be my husband's wife Be my children's mother
What has God entrusted to me?	The care of a home The care of children A ministry of writing

Am I a good steward of what I already have?	Do I manage money well? Do I care for my home? Do I love my husband and children the way I should? Do I work as effectively as I can?
What passion has God put in my heart?	To worship him To encourage women to be all they can be
What has God asked me to do that I haven't done yet?	For years, I knew I was called to write, but I didn't pursue it

Working It All Out

Once you have a clear vision for your priorities, don't be surprised if it takes time to work it out. You may have to resign from certain responsibilities. Do that respectfully by fulfilling your obligation. Even once you know your priorities, there's still flexibility in how you apply that knowledge. Crafting your schedule takes work, and there's constant revision going on.

Sometimes God shuts doors. Do we accept the shut door as a "no"? Or is it a call to press on and find a creative solution? Knowing what to do next takes prayer and sometimes a retooling of that priority list.

All this to say, it isn't easy. To be a woman who lives according to priorities, I must frequently check my motives. I choose to pull my heart back to a place of submission when I want to run ahead. I'm learning to wait on God's confirmation of something rather than challenging him to stop me. It's a completely different way of thinking than I did fifteen years ago. But it's brought more peace in my life, and the life of my family, than any time management system or daily planner ever could.

Chapter Seven

Understanding the Whys of Disorganization

In addition to not being able to tie my shoes, pregnancy with my third son Robbie hindered cleaning up after the other two. There was only so much picking up an eighteen-month-old and three-year-old were going to do. And since a toddler's job description includes leaving a trail of toys wherever he goes, my house was a double-the-fun disaster.

A few months later, another organizing challenge was born, literally. Robbie was a loving and opinionated baby from the start. He decided he much preferred being held by me to any other pastime, but only while I was walking or bouncing. Bottles and babysitters weren't an option because of his preference for me. He was ten months old before he slept through the night or took a bottle. He also didn't get out of diapers until three-and-a-half. He followed in his brothers' footsteps in that regard . . . bless his heart.

I have decided God put me on this earth, and gave me those three little boys, so that everyone else would feel good about themselves and their early parenting experience. Sigh.

As I've mentioned earlier in the book, motherhood rattled every-thing I knew, or thought I knew, about myself. I went from organized to disorganized and then more disorganized with every child. My physical and mental energy was sapped. My financial and personal resources were strapped. It was what organizing experts call "situationally disorganized." Something changed in my life, and disorganization followed.

Situationally Disorganized

This definition applies to many women reading this book. They have most of the skills and knowledge needed to bring order to their lives. They simply need to adapt what they already know to their current situa-tion. Or, they need to give themselves grace and ride it out.

Having children wasn't the only time I've fallen into a place of disor-ganization. When my father was dying, I set aside my regular responsi-bilities during the last month of his life. I've spent time intensely caring for my daughters, including homeschooling and uncovering cognitive disabilities and an attachment disorder. Facing a big deadline requires a similar myopic focus. There are times when needs or situations require the emotional energy or time we would normally distribute more evenly through the rest of our lives.

Sometimes wonderful happenings take our full attention, like a birth or a marriage. We are out of balance, and it's the right thing to do at the time. It is better to live with a messy house than to regret missing any of life's magnificent moments.

At some point, we pick ourselves up and slowly return to a new normal. There's no map showing us how to get back to a place of bal-ance or a correct timeline for arrival. Each of us walks our own road. But we don't have to walk it alone. The Bible tells us that God freely offers himself to us. God longs to offer comfort, wisdom, and strength . . . his strength.

When I find myself in a place of situational disorganization, I'm usu-ally frustrated. I'm not frustrated with anyone in particular, except myself for not being able to pull it together. That's when I need to apply God's grace to myself. God doesn't judge me, and my harsh self-judgment only hinders my ability to move forward.

Knowing the cause of disorganization should remove undue pressure. It happens to all of us. It's normal, and at times, it's even healthy. If you have poured yourself into helping someone or finishing a big project, those were your priorities. You'll have time to recover.

The good news is that practical tips can help you get back to a place of order. You might just need a fresh look at your home or office, some new ideas, and some inspiration to get organized.

However, not every disorganized condition is due to life's normal happenings. Another type has a deeper root. It is called "chronic disorganization."

Are You Situationally Disorganized?

1. Have you experienced a death of a loved one or family member within the last six months?
2. Have you recently gone through a divorce?
3. Is a parent/relative/friend who has started downsizing or is experiencing a life transition using your home as a storage facility either short-term or for an uncertain length of time?
4. Have you changed jobs or careers within the past year?
5. Has your spouse been forced to relocate because of job requirements, leaving the rest of the family to prepare the move, with little or no help?
6. Have you recently moved to a new location, had to begin a new job with no time to properly unpack and find suitable places for your possessions?
7. Has a family member recently experienced a serious illness that occupies most of your waking hours, not permitting you to follow your previous routine that maintains order within your household?

8. Has a parent who is unable to care for him/herself had to move into your home, causing you to change your normal routine and consequently disrupt your everyday management schedule?
9. Has the birth or adoption of a child upset the balance of your life more than expected?
10. Has your company determined that you can use your home office for your projects, but you have underestimated your available space?

Text taken from *Restoring Order*® Copyright © 2006 by Vicki Norris. Published by Harvest House Publisherrs, Eugene, Oregon 97402. Used by Permission..

• •

Chronic Disorganization

For some people, there are constant, underlying conditions that seriously hinder getting organized. It's not a matter of lack of willpower or weak character. Some chronic conditions people can't overcome alone. If that's the case, professional help may be the answer—both to find the underlying cause and provide guidance and practical help.

According to the Institute for Challenging Disorganization (www.challengingdisorganization.org), the definition of chronic disorganization is "having a past history of disorganization in which self-help efforts to change have failed, an undermining of current quality of life due to disorganization and the expectation of future disorganization." In short, if you've been disorganized in the past, have tried to change on your own, and forecast similar unsuccessful results in your future, you may suffer from chronic disorganization.

Sometimes there's an underlying condition such as ADHD, fibromyalgia, or multiple sclerosis. Learning disorders, like dyslexia, can affect organization. Depression, anxiety disorders, or physical handicaps can also play a factor.

People with a chronic disorganization problem have some of these symptoms:

- It's been a problem for many years.
- It negatively affects relationships with others.
- It causes embarrassment or humiliation.
- The individual accumulates possessions beyond apparent usefulness or pleasure.

If you believe you may have chronic disorganization, visit the Institute for Challenging Disorganization's website for referral information. Practical help is important, but don't neglect spiritual support as well.

James 5:16 says, "Therefore confess your sins to each other and pray for each other so that you may be healed. The prayer of a righteous person is powerful and effective." Years ago, I dealt with a fear of breast cancer. When a fibrocystic change sent me into a tailspin, I didn't tell anyone. I was too embarrassed to admit the depth of my fear. When I read this verse, I discarded it, thinking my fear wasn't "sin." Yet God revealed that my pride in not telling anyone about my problem was the sin.

I immediately called some friends and confessed my fear, and God was faithful to bring peace. Never since has fear consumed my heart. And this biblical promise is the reason.

If your disorganization is causing negative emotions, please share these honestly with someone you trust. Ask this person to pray for you. It won't bring immediate order to your kitchen, but it will help to bring a spirit of peace and calm to your heart.

For a full list of causes of chronic disorganization and the full questionnaire, visit www.challengingdisorganization.org.

Sometimes our disorganization is not situational or chronic—it's just life's ongoing demands that wear us out. Sometimes, I'm just tired of making decisions, and I want a mental vacation.

Tired of Making Decisions

Making decisions at the grocery store wears me out. What type of toothpaste, deodorant, or hair gel should I buy? As an editor, wife, and mother, I make decisions all the time. Whether it's to accept or reject an article, find a place for the latest sports photos, or plan my day, it seems that someone is always asking for a decision, and some days I'm just plain tired of making them.

That attitude gets me into trouble, because delayed decision making always leads to disorganization. I sit on e-mails, hold off on responding to invitations, and let paper pile higher and higher. Lack of a decision is the main cause for most of my paper problems. I've got one inbox, and it often becomes a catchall for things I don't know what to do with. When that happens, I spread out the pile, and I make one decision at a time until the pile is gone.

There are some principles that help me ease decision-making anxiety. Realizing no decision is perfect helps me decide what to do with all my stuff. So, I remind myself:

- I may not have all the information I need to make an informed decision, and that's okay.
- I may make a bad decision.
- I can change my mind later (on most things).
- My opinion matters. God gave me the responsibilities I have for a reason.
- Choose people over projects, love over achievement. Every time.

I also have another personal challenge to getting and staying organized: lack of follow-through.

Lack of Follow-Through

For some people, disorganization doesn't stem from the overwhelming number of decisions made in a day. For some, the problem is as simple as lack of follow-through.

Follow-through is the hard part. Taking a brilliant idea and finishing well takes discipline. Discipline doesn't come naturally for most of us. It's a habit that must be cultivated in the little things before we apply it to goals and dreams for our lives.

I wonder how many truly brilliant, original, life-changing ideas have disappeared because their creators lacked follow-through.

The good news is we can learn follow-through. Success with small, solid, disciplined habits leads to achievement with greater projects. Which is why making your bed and being on time for church are important habits to master.

To end this chapter, I've included a devotion I wrote for *Encouragement for Today*, devotions by Proverbs 31 Ministries called "Why You Should Hang up Your Robe."

◇   ◇   ◇

My first instinct was to leave the clean, folded clothes on *top* of the dresser. Granted, my arms were filled with freshly laundered items, so it would have been difficult to open the drawer while balancing the stack. I had an excuse for leaving them on top. Didn't I? Instead, I pushed past my instinct, took thirty more seconds, and placed the clothes neatly in the drawer.

This tendency *not* to complete a task happens with surprising regularity. I toss my bathrobe on the bed, drape jeans on the tub, and set the television remote on the nearest countertop. However, sometimes, when I'm a bit more self-aware, I take the five extra steps needed to actually finish the task.

Years ago, I realized that my practice of stopping short of finishing what I started led to a cluttered home and office. Back then, I had a multitude of unfinished tasks that I just lived with. It wasn't all simple things like putting away clothes, but included larger tasks like leaving a wall half-painted. I know that starting a project is fun, and it usually involves a burst of energy. Then, that energy wanes as I approach the finish line. Instead of pushing to complete the task, assignment, or project with excellence, I lean toward settling for good enough.

Unfortunately, when I settle for "good enough" consistently, I learn to live with mediocrity. And accepting mediocrity is far from where God

wants me to be. You see, finishing what we start is more than a good organizational or home management skill. It's also a spiritual discipline.

As I identified the tendency to settle, I realized it affected me in a
variety of ways throughout my life. In the past, I accepted a distant relationship with God rather than one of intimacy. I've limited my understanding of Scripture to a surface level. My relationships with others
have gone no deeper than, "Hi, how are you doing?" Instead of pushing
to explore the fullness of what God offers in all areas, it is easier to stop
short. Perhaps it's safer. It's simpler. And it causes less personal discom-
fort or inconvenience.

Interestingly, it's actually been somewhat simple to address this
issue. I admit the tendency within myself to settle, and I get firm with
myself about it. Now, when I would prefer to leave the dryer full of clothes
or the e-mail half-typed, I say to myself, "Finish what you start." I make
a conscientious decision to finish the task at hand before I move on to
something new. Obviously, there are some projects that require more
work, but this works on a lot of my issues.

I'm not sure of all the reasons for stopping short of finishing with
excellence, but I do know the results. I end up with a circle of unfulfilled
commitments, open loops, and shallow relationships. That's a far cry
from the life Jesus came to bring, which is full and abundant. It's not a
partial life or one that's hit or miss—it's lived by pushing to the limits and
exploring the outer reaches of life.

Maybe that seems a deep principle to pull from putting clothes in
a drawer or a dirty bowl in the dishwasher. However, the discipline of
finishing well is one that is woven through my life . . . or it's not.

So I guess I'll take the extra step and actually hang up my robe. It's
one more stitch in this tapestry of finishing well that God is trying to
create in my life.

It's Complicated

This chapter just touched the surface of the myriad reasons we get disorganized. I've found that if I give it serious thought, I can usually figure

out the reasons behind clutter or an overburdened schedule. Honesty is required: both to identify the source of the problem and to get help when needed.

Section Three

Jump-Start for the Seriously Overwhelmed

Chapter Eight

Simplify Your Schedule First

Have you ever noticed that some people accomplish more in a day than others do in a week? These same people remember birthdays, meet deadlines, and achieve goals. I know a few of these women and it's impressive.

You've probably wondered if they have more hours in their days than you. Have they figured out how to multitask while asleep? Do they have a staff of helpful oompa loompas? Are they bionic? Cloned? How do they do it?

The truth is we all have the same number of hours in our days. I'll admit, some women do have more energy and natural ability to order their days. And some have help. But we all have the same opportunity to manage our time effectively.

Regardless of your available time, energy level, and resources, you have everything you need to accomplish the responsibilities God has given you. The most important part of that last sentence is "the responsibilities God has given you." Not what *you* wish you could do. And not what your neighbor, sister, friend, or women's ministry director is able to do.

Focusing on what God is asking you to do today, this week, and this month is the first step in becoming a woman who manages time well. For most of us, this means simplifying our lives.

Too many women assume more responsibility than they should. The reasons are many and complicated. We love the excitement of a new project, the challenge, and the busyness of it all. Then we get to a breaking point and wonder how in the world we let it get this bad.

Consequently, we end up feeling drained, overwhelmed, resentful, and ready to quit anything and everything. And we don't want that! You can live a simple life with clear priorities and the right amount of responsibilities.

This chapter walks you through a simple approach to seeing your responsibilities with new eyes and implementing a basic system of managing them all.

It's a three-step process:

Step One: Personal assessment
Step Two: Edit your responsibilities
Step Three: Establish a review process

Step One: Personal Assessment

Have you ever avoided finding out the truth? I have. For some bizarre reason, I think if I don't step on the scale, I haven't gained any weight. Or, if I ignore the ache in my tooth, I won't need a root canal. Problem is, avoidance techniques only make matters worse.

To start becoming a better manager of your time, I'm going to ask you to do something painful. Not as painful as stepping on a scale, but close. Take a personal assessment of all your responsibilities, projects, priorities, and tasks. Everything. Capture it all on paper or on your computer. I promise you will feel better after it's done. Before I tell you how, I'll tell you why.

For years, I lived with an ongoing sense that I *should* be doing something at all times. It ate at me. Even when I was focused on something important, there was a latent unease about what *else* I should be doing. It wasn't until I read David Allen's *Getting Things Done* that I discovered a reason for my stress.

Allen writes, "The big problem is that your mind keeps reminding you of things when you can't do anything about them. It has no sense of past or future. That means that as soon as you tell yourself that you need to do something, and store it in your RAM (your mind), there's a part of you that thinks you should be doing that something all the time."[1]

It was a head-slapping moment when I read those words. That was it! Allen goes on to explain that the first step to finding a solution is to get everything out of your mind and store it somewhere safe. Not the "safe" place you stored an important document at home and now can't find. But somewhere close at hand.

I realized my mind was trying to manage more stuff than it could hold, and a to-do list wasn't the answer because it wasn't keeping things in safe places.

Think Like a Project Manager

For years, I tried to manage all my responsibilities on one to-do list. I tried to prioritize that to-do list using various methods, all without success. It was just too much to put on one sheet of paper . . . overwhelming, in fact. It was like trying to squeeze my size nine feet into cute little size six shoes. It wasn't happening.

I also never had an accurate view of all my responsibilities with one to-do list, and so I kept piling more on an overloaded schedule.

Instead of forcing my three-dimensional life onto a one-dimensional sheet of paper, I had to think outside the page and find another approach. There are many programs on the market to help people manage their responsibilities—too many to review in this book, though I mention a few digital programs in Chapter Fourteen. Pulling elements from excellent task management programs (like *Getting Things Done* by David Allen), I figured out how to capture all the stuff that caused underlying stress. I established two different types of lists: 1) projects and 2) tasks.

A *project* is anything that will take two or more steps. Right now, my personal project list includes things like this:

- Get graduation announcements for Dylan.
- Replace screens after hailstorm.
- Organize workshops for She Speaks.

Each of these projects takes multiple steps to complete, so they don't fit on a to-do list. By keeping them on a project list, they stay on my radar. I also can make notes about what I need to do and track progress.

To develop your own list, start by listing all the pending projects on one page. However, some projects need more space. So you might choose to put each project on its own page, especially those that are more complicated. This way, you can brainstorm and capture tasks required to complete the project.

A second list will be your *task* (or to-do) list. These items only take one step, such as "give books to Laura" or "make dentist appointment." You might choose to group like items here, too, such as errands, phone calls, or writing assignments.

My guess is these two lists will take you days, maybe weeks, to complete. Keep them handy so you can add to them as you remember things. Once you've captured all of your responsibilities in one place, you are ready for step two.

Create Your Own "Project Management" System

- Buy a three-ring binder, tabbed inserts, and lined notebook paper.
- Label tabbed inserts: "Tasks" and "Projects."
- Start listing your projects on one sheet of paper.
- Use a single page for projects that have multiple tasks.
- List all tasks that fall under each project.
- Assign deadlines for each task.
- Transfer items needing immediate attention to your task list.

Step Two: Edit Your Responsibilities

When all of your responsibilities and pending tasks are in one place, you can no longer avoid the reality of your schedule. If you feel overwhelmed most of the time, you probably have more responsibilities than you can handle, or you are spending time in the wrong places.

If that's you, you may need to edit your responsibilities. Even if they are good. Even if you are gifted for them. You probably need to delete some and redefine or reassign others. Here's an example from my own life.

I have the spiritual gifts of administration and leadership. I have usually taken the initiative when there's a need for leadership. In fact, even when there wasn't a need, I created one. When I was a little girl, I started clubs in the neighborhood. Once there was the Flower Club, and then the Good Deeds Club. Of course, I was always the president, and I would make little folders for all my club members. I loved it, but apparently no one else did, because my clubs never lasted long.

Fast forward to a time when my pastor asked if I would serve on the church's governing board. "Of course I would," I answered without spending time in prayer. It wasn't long before I realized it wasn't the best position for me.

Although I could handle the administrative work, my spirit was suffering. I found my heart hardening about certain situations. Business details filled my mind when I should have been worshipping. I was gifted, but I wasn't called. After a year, I resigned.

To edit and simplify your schedule, you'll need to do the following two things.

Identify Your Priorities

In Chapter Six, I shared my process for determining priorities. To summarize, I ask myself a series of questions, such as: "What can only I do?" and "Am I a good steward of what I already have?" If you haven't done that, I encourage you to spend some time considering the questions. You'll need to know your priorities to edit your schedule.

Some priorities are a given. For example, if you are a Christian, your faith is your number one priority. No other person can pursue a relationship with Jesus for you. Chapter Six outlines other priorities that are important for a well-balanced life.

But after those, you have some choices. Ask God for wisdom and search your heart for what truly matters to you in this world. What are your dreams? What ache is in your heart? What have you neglected? What has God asked you to do? These are your priorities. As you focus on your priorities, the next part of editing will be obvious.

Delete Some Things

Here's where it gets tough. If you really want to simplify your schedule, you will need to eliminate certain responsibilities.

You probably said yes to most things on your schedule because you *wanted* to do them. You might love singing in the choir, leading a committee, or volunteering for a local food bank. Making a decision to give any of them up will be difficult.

God may have truly called you to those assignments years ago. However, just because you were called to work in a job five years ago doesn't mean you are still called today. Just because you have the gift of teaching doesn't mean you are to be teaching *this* class.

After I had the boys, I continued with my life as if nothing had changed. I was overwhelmed, overwrought, and frustrated most of the time. Why wouldn't my children sit still? Why couldn't I go shopping like I used to without using food as a bribe? Why didn't they walk . . . anywhere? Why couldn't I *think*?

I was miserable. They were miserable. We were *all* miserable. God intervened in a dramatic way and moved me two thousand miles away from all my responsibilities. No work. No church. No extended family. No friends. There he overhauled my heart and schedule.

When our daughters joined our family in 2005, I decided to step back from most responsibilities for at least three years. What a difference *that* approach made. God clearly called us to adopt, but it was rough. If I hadn't edited my schedule, it would have been harder.

Editing your life is a process. It takes time to resign or redefine certain responsibilities. As you review your current schedule, consider the questions I've listed on this page about deleting responsibilities. They aren't definitive questions, but they can act as a guide. Sometimes God keeps me in a difficult situation somewhere to refine me, and I really need to change something inside me.

When to Delete a Responsibility

- When you know you aren't called to it.
- When your capacity to love those closest to you is diminished.
- When unkind thoughts fill your heart.
- When the joy you used to feel is replaced by resentment.
- When it's holding you back from pursuing God's new call on your life.

Tips for Simplifying Your Schedule

- Learn to say no.
- Wait a week before saying yes to a new responsibility.
- Pray about new opportunities, and ask God to confirm them. Wait until he does.
- Ask your spouse for his blessing before saying yes.
- Schedule less than you think you can do every day.
- Plan something fun every day.
- Make a menu for the week.
- Go shopping once a week.

Step Three: Establish an Ongoing Review Process

Capturing and editing all of your responsibilities isn't the end of this process. Without an ongoing review process, you'll slip back into your overwhelmed ways. No one drifts into an organized life. It takes ongoing discipline.

About once a week, I review pending projects. I think through everything I need to do, assess deadlines, and create a new task list.

I will always be busy, but I'm not overwhelmed. I rest easy knowing I've got my core responsibilities recorded and a plan to work through my tasks. If God changes my priorities, and he might, I'll be ready to get out my red pen and do some editing.

Chapter Nine

Remove the Clutter

There is always a cost of clutter. I've paid for it in tears, frustrated words, and wasted time. One morning in particular stands out in my memory as complete chaos. My cluttered schedule collided with a cluttered house, and in thirty minutes I went from being in control to having a meltdown. It started as a normal weekday morning. Everything was running smoothly until some last-minute needs tripped me up.

At 7:45, with thirty-five minutes to departure, third-grade Dylan reminded me he was Super Star of the week and needed to bring in a poster filled with baby photos. How could I have forgotten? I rushed around the house looking for photos and grabbed some from a messy pile in the office.

As we sat on the floor sorting through photos, Joshua told me he had volunteered to help decorate for a party at 8:00. He'd mentioned the party earlier in the week—when he told me he was bringing thirty-two gallons of orange juice! After I explained that would cost about ninety dollars, which was steep for a school event, we settled on something more affordable. In the hubbub about the juice, I neglected to write down the date of the party.

Well, it was that day. We raced to the car, leaving Dylan with a mess on the floor, and I pushed the automatic door opener. It started to open, then ground to a halt as a bike fell against it. By that time, it was 8:10, Josh was late, and the other two needed to leave in ten minutes. We cleared the obstacle and were starting to leave as I heard the phone ring. Dylan answered it and yelled into the garage, "It's the school. They wanted to know if you are coming. I told them you were on your way."

I had no idea why the school would be wondering if I was coming, and I was already frustrated. Assuming the call had something to do with the party, I turned to Josh and spoke in an elevated and annoyed voice, "*What* did you volunteer me to do at the party? Why is the school expecting me?" In the two-minute drive to school, I launched into a full-blown lecture on why Josh should never volunteer me for anything before he talked with me. He got out of the car without a kiss and shuffled off, shoulders hunched.

I raced home to get the other two boys out the door, late. How I wished I could have collapsed on the couch with a cup of coffee, but the morning wasn't over. In fact, I had fifteen minutes to get to church for a Bible study, for which I was taking snacks and leading a small group discussion. Unfortunately, I still wasn't ready.

As I raced to my bedroom, I glanced at the calendar and froze. There it was, an 8:00 meeting with my youngest son's speech therapist. *That* was the phone call from the school! The speech therapist, the homeroom teacher, and the assistant principal were waiting for me to show up. The worst part was they thought I was on my way.

I instantly burst into tears. Not just the sad, slow-drip-down-the-face kind, but sobs. Sobs that came from feelings of inadequacy and being completely overwhelmed. I was frustrated that I hadn't looked at my calendar and that I hadn't avoided the "emergencies" by preparing the night before. But more than anything else, I was devastated that I had lectured my sweet Joshua because I thought he'd done something wrong.

I made it to the study late, with red blotchy eyes, and later that day apologized to my children. But my emotions were wrecked. That day was lost to me, except for the lesson I learned: Clutter has a price. Sadly, everyone pays when I'm disorganized. That day serves as a perspective point for me. I remember it when I don't feel like addressing the clutter in my life.

Cost of Clutter

Not only is there an emotional cost of clutter, but there is a monetary expense to living with more than we can manage—whether it's in our homes or schedules. Consider these interesting facts about the cost of clutter:

- "National studies have shown that the typical executive spends four and one-half hours a week looking for lost papers. At a salary of $30,000, the cost of searching for important papers, measured in lost time, is $3,376 per year."[1]
- "According to management engineers, misfiled documents cost between $61 and $122 to be retrieved."[2]
- "Workers lose 280 hours per year, or seven weeks, seeking clarification because of poor communication due to disorganization."[3]
- If you ate out one meal a week because of a disorganized kitchen, it would cost approximately $25 for two, times 52 weeks, equals $1,300 a year in additional expenses. And that's a conservative estimate.

We don't need experts to tell us clutter costs. Any woman who has three bottles of pumpkin pie spice sitting next to five cans of poultry seasoning knows it can add up. We can't put a monetary value on time and energy, but looking for things around the home is clearly a waste of both.

Clutter Numbs Us

Sadly, we become immune to the clutter around us. Psychologists call it sensory adaptation. It's how people can work in a dairy farm or a perfume shop. After awhile you don't smell it anymore. The same thing happens to us—we become desensitized.

Seth Godin, author of *Tribes* and *Linchpin*, said this in a daily blog post:

> As digital marketers seek to increase profits, they almost always make the same mistake. They continue to add more clutter, messaging and offers, because, hey, it's free.
>
> One more link, one more banner, one more side deal on the Groupon page.
>
> Economics tells us that the right thing to do is run the factory until the last item produced is being sold at marginal cost. In other words, keep adding until it doesn't work anymore.
>
> In fact, human behavior tells us that this is a more permanent effect than we realize. Once you overload the user, you train them not to pay attention. More clutter isn't free. In fact, more clutter is a permanent shift, a desensitization to *all* the information, not just the last bit.[4]

If Godin is right, and I think he is, then clutter in our offices desensitizes us to clutter in our homes, which numbs us to clutter in our schedules. It's like an automatic force field. We shut out all information and sensory input as protection for our overloaded system. To counteract that, we must simplify. We must get rid of the extra stuff weighing us down. And we need help to break it down into manageable steps.

The rest of this chapter walks you through a five-step process to evaluate and bring order to areas of clutter in your life. While the process applies mostly to tangible clutter, we can also apply it to the intangible: our schedules. Hopefully this chapter will help establish a decision-making grid for even your most resilient clutter problems.

Professional organizers everywhere use these steps. The wording might change, but the process is logical and proven to work.

Step One: Group Like Items

Pick an area to work on and put similar items in grouping. For example, if you decide to organize your family room, start gathering items like remote controls, books, magazines, and DVDs. Continue this process until you've got every stray item in a pile of similar items. If you find things that belong in another room, then that becomes its own pile. Don't worry about what to do with it now. That comes next.

If you are applying this process to your schedule, consider grouping similar tasks, such as errands, phone calls, or responding to e-mails. This is why our grandmothers washed on Mondays, ironed on Tuesdays, and so on. It was a logical way to group tasks.

Step Two: Remove the Excess

When you realize that you have a stack of videocassettes, but no VCR, or a remote that doesn't go with anything you own, then you can safely decide to remove those items from your possession. Seeing all your items in logical groupings opens your eyes to reality. This happened when I reorganized my kitchen pantry once and realized I had enough oatmeal to make cookies for everyone at my children's school. I just kept buying more because I thought we were out.

Identifying duplicate items is only one reason to remove the excess. Hopefully, you'll identify items you don't like, don't want, or just don't need. Try to remove emotion, or unrealistic optimism, from your decision making.

When you find items you no longer want, store them together in a box or bin. Then plan to either give them away or sell them. For now, remove them from the area.

Removing the excess from your schedule takes some thought. I've addressed how to identify priorities in a previous chapter, and how to simplify your schedule in the next.

Step Three: Place and Replace

After you've grouped your items and removed the excess, it's time to put them where they belong, or find a permanent home for them. Some things just need to be put back. Hair products go in the bathroom, and books go on a bookshelf. That's easy.

You'll need to establish homes for other things. As you do, follow the general rule of storing items close to where you use them. For example, if you read magazines in your bedroom, then store them there.

This seems to be the hardest step. Some things remain strewn around your home because you simply don't know where to put them. I realize there isn't always an easy answer. Your closets and drawers might be stuffed. If so, consider stopping your current project and shifting your work to those areas.

You might need to purchase pieces of furniture to store your items. If finances are tight, consider shopping yard sales, Craigslist, or consignment stores. Let your friends know what you need. You never know who might want to sell something, or better yet, barter for something you have.

Step Four: Store Items in Containers

Containers, such as baskets and boxes, allow you to keep similar items together in a larger space. For example, if you have lots of seasoning packets, you might put them all in one stackable box. Or, partially used bags of pasta could go in a basket. You probably already do this in some areas of your home. Consider how you can apply this principle to other areas of your home.

For years, my husband travelled for work and brought home small, travel-sized containers of personal products. To keep them organized, I decided to put them in inexpensive plastic drawers. I measured my space and bought two sets of drawers at Target. Labels on each drawer completed the project, and those little bottles were neatly stored. The extra drawers hold simple first-aid supplies for minor scratches. This practice of storing items in containers makes life much easier.

Take accurate measurements of your available space, and assess the number of items to store. Planning beforehand will save time returning items that don't fit or aren't big enough to hold all you want to store.

Step Five: Assess and Maintain Regularly

Consider your initial attempt at organizing as a first draft. You will have to edit and re-edit. If something isn't working for you, try something else. What matters is that it helps you live a more ordered and peaceful life.

Maintenance is a daily practice and discipline that you can learn. Develop good habits of putting things back immediately after use. Just don't get discouraged with yourself when clutter accumulates again. Like any skill, it takes practice.

The second law of thermodynamics (a branch of physics) states: Without outside influence, all systems tend toward disorder. Although I am not a scientist, I can easily understand this principle. If I don't work daily to straighten my home, in less than twenty-four hours, it can turn into a disaster area. Managing clutter takes work. But the results of an ordered home and schedule are worth it.

Chapter Ten

Where to Start

Are you the type who has to have a plan before starting a project? The problem is you are too busy to create the plan, so the project never gets started. Or, does the idea of even starting to get organized overwhelm you? If so, this is the chapter for you.

I know what it's like to not know where to start. Sitting on my couch, having a mini-panic attack, I was in the middle of one of those days. I was drowning in to-dos, but I couldn't figure out what to do next. It was as if I were an airplane circling the city, hoping for the storm to pass so I could land. Only the storm was in my mind.

Thankfully, since that day, new systems and practices have helped bring my emotional responses under control. Most of the time, it's not a lack of skill or expertise to organize that hinders me. It's my emotional state. It's easy to feel burdened by responsibilities, victimized by circumstances, and frustrated by interruptions. Those emotions hinder us from pursuing our goals of establishing order and bringing peace into our lives.

My best response when detrimental emotions threaten is to either fall back on my established plan or create a plan. A plan is a lifeline when drowning in to-dos. Just knowing it's there helps me pause and reverse unproductive thought processes. My hope for this chapter is to help you do the same. I want to help you have a workable plan so you don't give up when frustration threatens.

If you can't even think of what to do next, don't despair. There's help for that, too.

The Art of "What to Do Next"

If you don't know what to do next, do nothing. That's right. Nothing. Sit for a moment and think. Take a deep breath. Say a prayer, asking for direction. Then wait with expectation. God will answer you. You may get an assignment or inspiration. Be patient; it's a good discipline.

You can ignore this step and just do something. Anything. That works sometimes, especially when you don't really have any deadlines or people expecting something from you. Just doing something works when it's a lazy Saturday morning, filled with undirected time. Or, if it's an emotionally draining time, keeping busy can be healthy.

Honestly, with five kids at home, I seldom have undirected time. God created me with a high level of energy and focus, and I channel those into projects most of the time. I've worked hard at the art of what to do next.

When I'm mentally overloaded, pausing to think and pray is the best use of time; in fact, it's an art. It's art because it allows me to create mentally. As I get direction, I add to my project and task lists. I immediately put those ideas into writing. Many people benefit from journaling. While I'm not a journal writer, I see the benefit in capturing thoughts and ideas without worrying about structure. If that's you, keep a journal with you at all times and write your thoughts as they come to you. Worry about order later.

David Allen, author of *Getting Things Done*, says this about taking time to think: "[T]hinking in more effective ways about projects and situations can make things happen sooner, better and more successfully."[1] Really, thinking is an underestimated art.

Nurturing this art will tap your mental potential. You have creativity inside you because you were created in the image of God. Put yourself in pause and allow creativity to develop.

As you think and pray, you will know how to progress with getting organized. In this chapter, I've presented approaches which might help you. The bottom line is to approach organization in a manner that best suits you at this time in your life. There is no right or wrong way. However, I do recommend you consider starting with your schedule.

Start with Your Schedule

My kids know the crazy-woman look that comes over me at times. It usually happens when I'm rushed. I make mistakes, forget things, snap at little annoyances, and generally make everyone unhappy. Including the dog. That is not the woman I want to be.

The woman I want to be creates a schedule that allows for margins around appointments, plans ahead, allows enough time for projects, and has enough white space for emergencies. For the most part, I am the designer of my schedule. Even in situations where others dictate requests, I still control how they are managed.

If life has taken a different turn than you expected, you can't control that. But you still have the intelligence and creativity to adapt with graciousness. I've covered tips for simplifying your schedule in Chapter Eight and managing time in Chapter Eleven which can help in managing your schedule.

The reality is that without control over the intangible parts of life (managing your schedule, projects, and tasks), you'll struggle with control over the tangible (your home and office stuff). If you don't have the time to manage your paper, pay your bills, or reorganize your closet now, you never will. You won't wake up one day with a manageable schedule!

Once your schedule is under control, planning won't seem impossible. If your schedule is already manageable, but you feel overwhelmed by the physical acts of breaking down the task in front of you, I've included some ideas on how to get started.

Divide and Conquer

Let's say you can't find your living room couch under all the clutter. If I told you in the midst of your chaos, "Go organize your living room!" you would laugh in my face. I would deserve it, too. Because we both know you would have done it if you could.

But if I suggested you gather all the old newspapers and put them in a recycling box, you could manage that.

Tackling a big project takes the same approach. It's simply breaking down a big task into little tasks logical to you. We do this type of strategizing in real life all the time. If you want to plan a vacation, you'll need to arrange a flight or driving plan, a place to stay, activities, and meals. The bigger the vacation, the more detailed the planning.

This is no different. No one can just "get organized" without some kind of plan. What that plan looks like is completely up to you.

A Master Plan Approach

My first job out of college was for a land developer. They had a 180-acre master planned community to develop. They drafted an original plan before I joined their staff, and they were actively building different projects. It was exciting to see the map and envision the retirement center planned on one ten-acre plot and the medical offices on another. It was even more thrilling to be there at a grand opening of something we'd worked on for years.

Although the master plan took a long time to create, it became an invaluable guide once it was complete. A similar master planning mode can help if you prefer a comprehensive approach. You'll need a vision for each area of your home you want to change and some ideas. A lot of the details can wait. Following are some ideas for creating a master plan for organizing.

Create an Organizing Notebook

You might like to keep all your notes and plans in one place. If so, consider creating your own organizing notebook with these simple tips:

- A spiral notebook or three-ring binder will work for those who like things on paper. You can also use a computer.

- Assign several pages for each project within your home. A project could be a room, or it could be specific areas or projects like: books, closets, clothes, toys.
- On each page, create a list of initial tasks. (Example: sort children's books, research who accepts donations of children's books, take children's books to library.)
- Leave room for more tasks as you develop the plan.

Once you've got a notebook created, start your research for products or furniture you might want to buy. Keep lists of stores and prices. Paste pictures of ideas from magazines and links to interesting websites. This notebook will be your guide as you work through each area of your office and home.

From your master plan, identify one project to tackle first. From that project list, identify the next action needed to move the project forward. Continue with this approach until you've successfully achieved your organizing goals.

Sample Project Notebook Page
Master Bedroom (including closet)

To do

- Throw away or recycle all stray papers
- Put books into bookshelves
  - o Sort by type of book
- Sort through clothes
  - o Put winter clothes in storage boxes
  - o Give away out-of-style dress clothing
  - o Give away too-small clothes
  - o Throw away broken shoes, purses, and belts
- Sort through dresser drawers
- Find a place for exercise clothes
- Clean out bedside table

- Vacuum under bed
- Hang up pictures currently on top of dresser
- Launder comforter

To buy

- Dividers for dresser drawers
- Bedside table with drawers
- Two under-the-bed storage boxes
- Shoe keeper for over the closet door
- Organizer for jewelry
- Desktop valet

Create a Week-by-Week Guide

Setting goals and deadlines is a great way to keep on task with your organizing. You can create your own week-by-week guide by adding another section to your organizing notebook.

First, decide how much time you can spend on organization in a normal week. If it's two hours, then identify tasks that take approximately that much time.

If you would like to have your home organized by Christmas, and it's June, then create a twenty-four-week schedule. Your weekly schedule might look like this:

Week 1: Organize food in kitchen
Week 2: Organize drawers and cabinets in kitchen
Week 3: Organize hall closet
Week 4: Organize linen closet
Week 5: Organize master bathroom

If you miss a week due to unexpected activity or illness, then pick up where you left off. A schedule isn't supposed to cause you extra guilt if you get off-task. It's a tool to help you stay on task—that's all.

If creating your own guide is too much work, I recommend the book *Organize Now!* by Jennifer Ford Berry. It's a handy little book with a year-long plan for organizing everything from your schedule to special events, like holidays, parties, and back-to-school time. She's included room for notes and a checklist for each week.

A Task Approach

If a master plan is too much to manage, consider a task-by-task approach. This still requires some planning, but instead of creating a master plan, you'll work on one project at a time. Give some thought to what order makes the most sense. Following are some suggestions.

Start at the front entrance. If you feel overwhelmed the moment you walk in your home, then start at the front entrance. Establish a tidy, clean, and organized space to set the mood and say "welcome home."

Start with what causes the most pain. What bothers you most in your life? What causes anxiety every time you see it? If your hall closet takes two people to shut the door, and it's driving you nuts, you might want to start there. If you are sleeping on the couch because extra clothes are covering your bed, start there. Eliminate sources of stress and frustration first, and you'll feel encouraged to continue.

Start with what will give you the most immediate gratification. Starting with an easy task will provide immediate gratification. That gratification will feel so good, I'm confident you'll be motivated to keep going. Areas that tend to provide immediate gratification are kitchen and bathroom counters and office desktops.

Start with what must be done first. Often, an external deadline is quite an effective motivator. If guests are coming for Thanksgiving, you will want to work on the guest room and bath. If you are hosting a birthday party, start with the living room. If you are expecting a baby, start with the nursery. External motivators and short deadlines can be our friend. When my husband and I are approaching a deadline, we laughingly say, "If it wasn't for the last minute, some things would never get done."

Just Start

If a task approach is still too much for you at this point in your life, then just start somewhere. Schedule a block of time to work—an hour would be a good amount of time for you to accomplish something. Then start with a small project, like a junk drawer or your pantry. Focus on one small task you can complete in an hour.

As you become more confident, consider adding more structure to your planning. It's not a requirement, but it's a practice that will help see you through to the end result you desire—which is greater order and peace.

Simple Steps to Creating Order

Chapter Eleven

. . . .

Time Management

. . . . ⤖ . . . .

I'm thinking about starting a petition to ask God for more hours in a day. Twenty-four sounds like enough, but really it isn't. First, I've got to sleep for at least seven of those. Then there's work, shopping, cooking, laundry, housecleaning, volunteering at church, helping with my children's school, homework, making lunches, and so on. Somehow in the midst of all that, I'm supposed to care for myself. And how could I not put time with God first on that list? Do you have a pen for that petition?

It's not like I'm telling you something you don't know. Most of us could use a few more hours in our days . . . energetic, high-focus hours, if you please. Finding time to do it all is a myth. This is why so many people have held a grudge against the Proverbs 31 woman for millenniums. A cursory review of that biblical chapter shows a woman who is sewing, selling, and saving, all while her husband brags on her in town and her children bow at her feet.

It's those servants she had, we say with disgust. If we had a few, we'd accomplish as much. I was reminded a few years ago that we actually do have servants these days, the electric kind: dishwashers, washing machines, and dryers. I stopped complaining.

The truth is, we don't all have the same amount of energy, the same body clock, or common talents. We have differing emotional reservoirs and tolerances. What I can push through emotionally would detour another's day. That's why evaluating how we manage time wasters, and how we make the most of our day, is uniquely personal. And comparing ourselves to each other is deadly.

You can manage time wisely and accomplish what you are supposed to do in the time you have been given. The key to that last sentence is the "what you are supposed to do." If you are a mother of small children, and you are frustrated that you can't attend meetings at night, perhaps you should stop attending meetings at night. Maybe that's not what you are supposed to do.

If you are constantly behind schedule, underperforming, angry, making mistakes, or late, then something needs to be changed. Here are some examples of common time management problems:

- Saying yes to things you shouldn't.
- Not differentiating between urgent and important.
- Allowing too many unnecessary interruptions.
- Using time inefficiently.

The good news is all of this can change. I've addressed the issues of how to say no, setting reasonable expectations, and identifying priorities in Chapters Three, Four, and Five. If you skipped those, I encourage you to go back and read them. I don't blame you for skipping to this chapter. It's what I would do, too. But without being grounded in these areas, all the time management tips in the world won't solve the problem.

In this chapter, I'm going to dig into some practical tips for making the most of our time. Before we start good habits, however, we have to stop bad ones. The first part of the chapter will address time stealers and other habits that hinder productivity. The second half will include tips on making the most of our time.

Identifying Time Wasters

Productive women maintain focus. If you were a fly on the wall watching a highly organized woman, you would discover that she squeezes out every drop of effectiveness from her day. That doesn't mean she's always working. She knows when to rest and play. She's able to minimize distractions and time stealers and be about her business.

Today, we have more time wasters than ever before. They are traps in our day, waiting to snare us and redirect our attention from priorities. They aren't detrimental on their own. They become problems, however, when they keep us from achieving our goals.

Here's a personal example. Reading magazines inspires me. I love home decorating and cooking magazines. However, if I'm facing a deadline or my children have asked for help, it can become a time stealer. Unless I'm reading for research or I've scheduled a break, I should postpone my reading pleasure until an appropriate time.

Think through and be honest about what steals time from your priorities. Some things will be obvious; others harder to identify. It's a little like starting to budget your finances. Say you begin the week with a hundred dollars, but by Saturday you have no money and nothing to show for it. Where did it go? Time is just like that. Instead of keeping track of every dollar, you might want to track minutes. Following are common time wasters.

Obvious

- Television
- Internet
- Phone calls
- Online games (solitaire)
- Interruptions
- Meetings

Not-So-Obvious

- Tasks you could have delegated
- Procrastination and indecision
- Requests of others

- Unclear communication
- Inadequate technical knowledge
- Unclear objectives and priorities
- Lack of planning
- Stress and fatigue
- Personal disorganization
- Crisis management
- Unhealthy friendships
- Worry

Once you've identified some of your time wasters, then you can work on stopping those before you try and start new habits.

Common Time Stealers and Solutions	
Television or Other Media	Record or DVR programs. Download podcasts to listen to while exercising. Get news on a Kindle or iPad and read while waiting.
E-mail	Review at set times during the day. Shut down e-mail server during other times. Announce to co-workers when you will check e-mail.
Social Media	Be realistic about how much time this takes. Schedule a time during the day to devote to it. Limit friends to people who are really friends.
Gossip	Decide to become a person who doesn't gossip, and you'll discover you have more time.
Responsibilities you aren't called to	Once you've identified your priorities, start to responsibly reduce your commitments.
Shopping	Make lists and stick to them.
Exhaustion	Have a medical checkup to determine possible underlying problem. Get to bed earlier.

When Is It Not a Time Stealer?

Some things are never time stealers for me. For example:

- Prayer
- Meeting my family's needs
- Meeting my emotional needs
- Showing love to others
- Exercise
- A trip to Starbucks

Although meeting my family's needs is on my list, there are times I don't drop everything to help. Sometimes my children need to experience the consequences of their choices.

Taking personal breaks is also critical to productive time management. My friend Lysa loves bubble baths. In fact, they help restore her energy and focus. A bath might be her most important task some days. That's what a trip to Starbucks does for me. Instead of being a drain on my time, knowing that I will soon be drinking a creamy sweet coffee drink is a motivation. Then, I get a boost of energy when I'm drinking it. In fact, I sometimes call it my liquid nap.

For the rest of this chapter, I've bulleted some simple time management tips. Adopting a few can make a big difference.

Time Management Tips

To gain control over your time, start making little changes. Five minutes saved here and there quickly add up to an hour. Then, you've got an hour to spend where you *want*—instead of looking for your cell phone. The more smart habits you develop, the less time you'll waste.

Tips for Home

- Keep small bills on hand. In my home, someone always needs a dollar or five-dollar bill.
- Create a weekly menu. (See Chapter Eighteen.)

- Always have backup dinner items in the freezer (pizza or frozen casserole).
- Put a basket by the front door for keys, sunglasses, wallets, and other often-lost items.
- Designate a basket for library books or items to return to others.
- Buy an address/phone book with lots of entry space. Record every phone number you think you might use. Record website usernames and passwords here as well.
- Record phone numbers for service providers by the type of service: computer repair, accountant, hair stylist, dentist, etc.
- Buy a headset that clips on your waistband for your home phone. Talk and work at the same time.
- Schedule your responses. My friend Karen Ehman, author of *The Complete Guide to Getting and Staying Organized*, has a home answering machine that doesn't accept messages. Callers hear a brief message telling them the Ehmans aren't available and the system isn't set up to accept a message. Callers are asked to try back at a later time. Karen uses caller ID to either return the call or let the caller try again.

Tips for Shopping

- Buy an extra item for those things you use most often (condiments, shampoo, lightbulbs, etc.)
- Maintain shopping lists in one place: grocery, general errands, Target, etc. As soon as you are out of something or identify a need, put it on the correct list.
- Don't go to the store without a list.
- Group your errands. Never run just one if possible.
- Don't let your gas tank go below half.
- Grocery shop and run errands in the morning when fewer people are out.

Tips for Managing Tasks and Appointments

- Schedule extra time for each daily activity. Everything takes longer than we think it will.
- Leave fifteen minutes earlier than you think you need to for an appointment. Return phone calls, read a book, or work while you wait.
- Use the alert function on your phone or electronic calendar to remind you about appointments and deadlines.
- Print out a map when going to a new place.
- Invest in a GPS system if you are directionally challenged.
- Carry a notebook to capture great ideas or things you need to do.
- Keep a voice recorder in the car.
- Listen to audio books during commute time.
- Take excellent notes when working with others. Record who is supposed to do what and by when. This will save time trying to track down this information later.

Catch-Up Tips

For one week, try the following:
- Get up an hour earlier each day.
- Give up your lunch hour at work.
- See how fast you can accomplish home cleaning. Side benefit of speed cleaning: you'll burn extra calories.
- Hire a teenager to run errands one Saturday.
- Barter childcare with a friend for a day.
- Cancel text messaging.

General Tips

- Don't be a perfectionist with everything. Some tasks don't require your best effort. Learn to distinguish between tasks that deserve to be done with excellence and tasks that just need to be done.
- Don't do other people's work. Learn to delegate effectively and teach others how to do their own work.
- Immediately clean up after yourself and put items away. If possible, don't set an item down after use. Put it away. For example, when cooking, measure the salt and put it back in the cabinet, not on the counter.
- If something takes a minute or two, do it right away.
- Learn shortcuts on your computer keyboard. Instead of reaching for the mouse, learn which keys do what. To find out, click on the help button and search "keyboard shortcuts."
- Work with excellence the first time to avoid a second time.
- Discover what works best for your unique personality and stick with it. Don't let any "expert" tell you what you should do.
- If something is not working, change it.

Develop a Weekly Routine

Spend some time at the beginning of each week to plan your schedule. Taking the extra time to do this will help increase your productivity and balance your important long-term projects with your more urgent tasks. Once a week:

- Review incomplete projects.
- Review upcoming deadlines.
- Set goals.
- Identify priorities for each day, or the week.
- Schedule time for yourself.

- Schedule time to show love or hospitality to others (planned acts of kindness).

Develop a Nighttime Routine

Doing a few things every night will ease your morning. Some great evening activities include:

- Review the next day's schedule, including meals.
- Write a daily to-do list based on priorities.
- Sign school papers and pack backpacks. Set by the door.
- Pack briefcase or tote bag and set by the door.
- Clean the kitchen.
- Decide on breakfast.
- Pack lunches.

We are stewards of our time, and we will be held accountable for our use of it. We should use it wisely and be about our Father's business. Yet, while I value productivity, I'm diligent to balance it with downtime and invest time in the people around me. My daily prayer is that I never get so consumed with my to-do list that I miss God's to-do list. That is my prayer for you as well.

Steps to Overcome Procrastination

- Have a brain dump session. Get everything connected with the resistant project out of your brain and onto paper.
- Break up the task into manageable chunks. Write down tasks on index cards. Then put them in the chronological order necessary to complete the assignment.
- Set short-term goals with due dates.
- Choose an easy task to start momentum.
- Reward yourself when you've met your due date.

Chapter Twelve

Setting Up an Organized Home Office

The line between work and home isn't blurred—it's obliterated. Given the increase in home-based businesses, telecommuting, and cute desk accessories, millions of us now have some sort of home office. Although few have the luxury of a dedicated room, most women create some sort of "office" center.

Even if you don't telecommute for work or run a home-based business, you need to manage more work and information than ever before, and a professional approach helps. Have you ever been asked questions like:

"Honey, do you know where our auto insurance information is?"
"Mom, where's the receipt for my iPod? It's broken again."
"Did you see that paper I brought home from church?"
"It's tax time again. What did we do with our medical receipts?"

If you are tired of saying "I don't know," or spending more time than necessary trying to accomplish a task, perhaps you need to evaluate your workspace and raise the professionalism of your approach.

In this chapter, we'll look at the basics of setting up an organized office center. This doesn't have to take up lots of space, but it needs to be a place where you can manage information, projects, tasks, and various responsibilities with ease. The principles will apply if you live in a tiny apartment and your "office" is a kitchen table, or if you have the luxury of an entire room. My office is a built-in desk under my stairs in my family room. Not where all the "experts" say it should be. But it meets my work needs.

Once you get this space established or redefined, you'll have a place to funnel those papers, notes, books, and lists scattered throughout your home. In the next chapter, we'll continue the discussion with more details on managing paper. For now, we'll create a space for it.

This chapter is written with the fundamentals in mind. Some women are still trying to manage their increased workload without proper equipment. If you just need tips for organizing your existing office, I've tucked those in as well. Hopefully there's a little something for everyone.

Identify Your Purpose

What type of work happens in your office? Do you need a phone, a computer, or places to store books and binders? Perhaps you are a crafter or digital scrapbooker. Is quiet time critical for important phone calls or teaching webinar classes? Or is it more important to be accessible to your family? Perhaps you don't need a desk as much as a table to spread out your papers.

One reason you might struggle to get organized is that you are trying to follow expert advice you learned long ago. But if that's not working for you, then let it go and start again. Identify your realistic purpose for this space and think through how to make that happen.

Locate and Set Up Your Space

Once you've identified the "what" of your office space, consider the "where" options. Don't settle on what makes the most "logical" sense. Think beyond solving your immediate needs to creating a place where you'll explode with productivity.

Be Creative

As you look around your current living space, identify all the options for setting up your office. Be creative and don't get hung up on traditional office settings. Here are some ideas:

- An unused closet.
- Under the stairs.
- In a guest room.
- A small secretary desk in the living room or kitchen.
- Built-in desk and shelving along a wall or in a nook.

If the perfect place doesn't exist, think about:

- Building out a portion of your garage.
- Converting a patio to usable room.
- Dividing a large room into two smaller rooms.
- Designing and building an adorable mini-cottage in your backyard. (I know that's going a bit far, but it's okay to dream.)

Consider Physical Needs

As you're looking for a place to locate your office, take the following into consideration:

- Access to electrical outlets.
- Glare on the computer screen.
- Access to cable outlet or outside wall for convenient installation.
- Access to walls for shelving, bulletin boards, or wall files.

Your Personal Style Matters

Your office should be a place of inspiration. For some that means ruffled comfort, for others streamlined and modern. What will bring you the most joy? Whatever your style, you are sure to find office furniture and accessories to match. For inspiration, www.hgtv.com has almost one hundred styles of offices. If you are in a position to invest in furniture, shop around before making a decision based on convenience.

Prioritize Your Filing System

The time you invest in creating filing systems will come back to you triplefold in time saved. In fact, this could be your strongest tool for staying on top of your workload. Most of us have two types of files: electronic and hard copy. This chapter addresses traditional files holding paper.

Files are the core foundation of most types of organization. Whether it's important documents, warranties, receipts, project summaries, sermon notes, or fundraising reports, most of us want to be able to access information when we need it. Yet without an adequate and organized filing system, we'll waste precious time searching for what we need.

As our lives become increasingly complicated, our need to access and archive different items changes. For example, we need immediate access to certain types of information, such as current projects and children's school information, while past tax returns can be archived. Mixing the two can be problematic for some.

If you've been trying to get by with one system, consider dividing your documents into active and archive files and putting them in different locations. In the next chapter, we'll dig deeper into the types of paper you'll need to file. For now, we'll discuss hardware and external organization.

As space allows, purchase the largest and sturdiest filing cabinets you can afford. You may be tempted to purchase the smallest one necessary, but if you do, you will hesitate to use it for fear of filling it up. Also, stay away from the cheapest option. The glides may work now, but once filled with files, its weakness will be evident.

Setting Up Your Files

Having enough of the right supplies will ease your filing. If you only purchase a dozen files and you really need a hundred, you'll be frustrated at the get-go. Following are some helpful purchases and suggestions on how to use them.

Hanging Files

Hanging files are generally used for major categories of filing. Categories might include:

- Automobile
- Finances
- Health
- Home Maintenance
- Insurance
- School

Letter-Sized File Folders

Letter-sized file folders sit inside hanging files. These files are often used for subcategories. Examples of subcategories include:

Category: Automobile
Subcategories: Could include one file for each vehicle, or if you only have one, you might have individual files for insurance, registration, and warranty.

Category: Finances
Subcategories: Checking account, savings account, credit cards, credit report, retirement, investments, etc.

Store extra files in your filing cabinet so they are easily available when you want to create a new file. Guard against overstuffing your file drawers. Jam-packed drawers will discourage you from daily filing or creating new files. Consider your files as an integral part of your home organization and invest in additional file cabinets when necessary. Purging your files every six to twelve months is a good practice.

Anything important can go in your files. They don't just have to be for documents. Consider filing any stray paper you don't know where to store, such as: sermon notes, Christmas cards, addresses, birthday cards, and ideas for future vacations. Simply identify a broad category, such as "Family Fun" or "Spiritual Growth" and start saving those important, but miscellaneous, pieces of paper.

Label Maker

A label maker not only makes your files look professional, but it will delight you visually. There's something about seeing freshly labeled files that makes me sit up just a little taller. Also, a consistent font style makes it easier to see at a glance what you are looking for.

Products to Help

If categorizing is difficult for you, consider purchasing a ready-made filing program. There are many companies producing ready-made files and labels to help you set up files and maintain organization. Here are some to research:

- EasyFile—www.easyfilesolutions.com
  Includes guidebook, color coded labels and tabs, and sample forms for everyday organization.
- Freedom Filer—www.freedomfiler.com
  This company offers several products but prides itself on its self-purging file system.
- Find-N-File—www.findnfile.com
  Includes options for color-coded files and labels, together or separate.
- JOYS (Just Organize Your Stuff)—www.justorganizeyourstuff.com
  Includes color-coded labels for the creative, left-brained thinker.
- Paper Tiger—www.thepapertiger.com
  This is a software system which allows for filing and

retrieval of documents by a word or category search. This is for more detailed filing systems.

Make It Ergonomically Correct

For years, I suffered with a sharp pain in my left shoulder blade after working for a few hours. Assuming it was a normal part of typing for a living, I took breaks, got back rubs, and accepted the minor pain.

It wasn't until my sister Liz, who is a purchaser for a major university, commented on the importance of ergonomics that I put two and two together. I was using the only desk we had at the time, and it wasn't designed for a computer. That meant the keyboard and mouse sat too high; consequently, I held my shoulders up, and my arms were at the wrong angle. Because I'm left-handed, my left shoulder blade hurt. Now that my keyboard is at a safe height, I type pain-free.

Without a corporate human resource department to watch out for potential OSHA violations, the home worker can easily overlook the physical dangers possible in an office environment. Following are some safety details you might want to consider as you create your home office.

Glare. Watch for direct and reflected glare on your monitor screen. If you find yourself tilting your head to see the screen, you have a problem. To avoid this, invest in a glare-free monitor and close the blinds on windows.

Monitor placement. To avoid other eyestrain issues, minimize the contrast between your screen and the background. Although facing a window can offer a lovely view, the bright background will cause problems. Consider putting your monitor against a wall.

Position the top of the monitor at about the same height as or lower than your eyes and at least twenty-five inches from your face. If you can place your monitor further away and still read it, that's even better.

Chair. Consider a chair that allows for a slight recline. Ergonomics consulting company Ankrum Associates, through their Workplace Ergo, Inc. website, recommends "the idea of a much wider hip angle, with 130 degrees or so as an 'optimum' angle."[1] The reason? When the hips are straightened, the vertebrae of the lower spine are aligned with each other in a way that reduces and evens out pressure on the intervertebral discs. Further, sitting upright is less desirable than reclining. When reclining, the lower back muscles work less and the spine supports less weight, since body weight is held up by the chair's backrest.

Shoulders, arms, and hands. Keep your elbow angle at ninety to one hundred degrees as you work with the keyboard, keeping your arms held close to your sides. Keep your wrists flat when you are typing. Consciously relax your shoulders and arms. Keep the mouse and keyboard as close together as possible to eliminate unnecessary reaching. A chair with adjustable armrests is a great investment.

Breaks. Intersperse your work with frequent breaks and movement. The University of California Los Angeles Ergonomics Department advises we "take one or two minute breaks every 20–30 minutes, and five minute breaks every hour. Every few hours, try to get up and move around."[2] Raise your arms, reposition your legs, or just stand to eliminate the stress on your body.

Invest in Yourself

Your work at home has value. First Corinthians 10:31 says, "So whether you eat or drink or whatever you do, do it all for the glory of God." As you seek to obey God's call on your life and bring him glory, consider making decisions that will increase your stewardship of your time, talents, and energy. I write this to encourage you to invest wisely in your home office and its equipment.

Investing in your calling is as valid, if not more valid, than investing in anyone else's ministry or calling. A lack of 501(c)(3) standing doesn't minimize your work. The reality is that much ministry happens at home. That might mean new, faster, sturdier equipment is required for efficient work. Whether you are helping your son with a school project or creating a calendar for nursery volunteers at church, if you are living according to God's priorities for you, then your work is critically important.

Stock your office with equipment that will last. Invest in an excellent computer, a printer or scanner, and solid desk accessories. Research your options carefully as one who carries the weight of God's calling. Prayerfully consider your purpose for your office and equipment. Create an environment where you can thrive in your calling to be a productive, organized worker at home.

Chapter Thirteen

Overcoming Paper Clutter

One would think managing paper wouldn't be a problem, given the advent of the digital age. But it is! Organizing stacks and piles, papers and files is an ongoing challenge for women—especially those who grew up pre-computer.

Years ago, I saved every piece of paper just in case. Every bill, receipt, and note from the teacher was tucked away—for years. If I ever needed to know how many times we changed the oil in our car, I would be ready. If we sold our car, wouldn't the buyer want to know that? Probably not.

It took years before I realized the paper I was trying to manage was really managing me. My paper-saving was fear-driven rather than based in the reality of our new electronic society. This same cautiousness causes many women to amass mountains of paper and drastically reduce usable counter space. Worse than the mess is the underlying anxiety from the visual clutter.

For that reason, my policy is no loose paper on any surface. Yet even with the best intentions, my piles grow. The reason is simple: I don't know where to put the different types of paper.

In this chapter, we'll evaluate the variety of paper entering our homes and strategize the best storage spots for each type. I'll also give you some guidelines on what to keep and what is safe to discard, plus ways to reduce paper for good. Most paper falls into one of five categories.

Pending: This would be invitations, school field trip permission forms, grocery store ads, schedules for sports or entertainment seasons, coupons, and recipes. We fear losing or forgetting them if filed, but they need to go somewhere.

Action and review: These papers are pertinent to a current project or are something you want to review. This could include a class syllabus, Bible study assignment, magazine, catalog, or project at work or church.

Everyday reference: These papers might include receipts and tax documents for the current year, warranties for new items, health information, or home maintenance records.

Long-term reference: You need these documents rarely, but you need to have them close at hand. These could include old tax documents or purchase information on older items.

Vital records: Documents that would be impossible or hard to replace should be kept safe. These include but aren't limited to birth, wedding, and death certificates, passports, social security cards, wills, savings bonds, etc.

Before you start to tackle your stacks, think through these different categories of paper and where you store them. You don't necessarily need five locations for storage, as some of these could be combined, based on the amount of paper you need to file. Categorizing helps to create order in your mind and in your home.

Handle Paper Once

Daily habits make a huge impact on managing clutter. Without a routine, you'll always end up with overwhelming piles. Creating a paper-processing center helps. This center is where you'll decide what to keep, what to shred, and what to recycle. Ideally, it would be next to your shredder and a recycle box.

Practice handling each sheet of paper once, and follow through until it's safely stored and easily accessed.

Pending, Action, and Review Files

Many families benefit from a tabletop file system for papers that fall in the pending or action categories. If you don't have room, consider putting these files in front of your household reference files. This system should contain individual files for the information you need most throughout the week. Here are some suggestions for files:

- Pending (you'll need these items very soon—directions to a play, invitation, flyer for an event, etc.)
- Bills to pay
- To-do lists
- A file for each family member
- Church (could contain sermon notes or calendar of events)
- Children's activities

Add or remove files regularly to ensure this filing system is up-to-date with your family's needs.

Everyday and Long-Term Reference Files

As you set up your filing cabinet, be selective in what you save. Getting and keeping every statement or receipt isn't necessary with the increase of online statements. If you still want the security of reviewing a paper statement, then shred documents once you've confirmed they are accurate.

In this next section, I've shared basic guidelines on what documents to keep and for how long. Please note this is *not* professional advice. Every family is different. Check with your accountant or visit www.irs.gov for more detailed information. Also, this list doesn't apply to self-employed individuals or businesses. It's also not a comprehensive list of everything you'll want to file.

Enough with the qualifications, here is some practical advice for general paper management:

Tax returns (and supporting documents): Keep for at least seven years.

IRA contributions: Keep deposit statements until you withdraw the money entirely. You need to show if you paid taxes when it's time to withdraw.

Receipts for purchases: If you purchased the item with a credit card, save the receipt until it has shown up correctly on the statement. Once you have been correctly billed, shred the receipt, unless:

- You need it for the warranty or service agreement. You might consider storing these receipts in your files under general categories like kitchen, computers, televisions, handheld electronics, and so on.
- It's an item of value. Then either keep the receipt or record the purchase price in a ledger in case you need it for an insurance claim due to theft or damage.
- It was for a gift or an item that might be returned. Save it until you are certain the item won't be returned.

Investment/banking/retirement statements: Keep the quarterly statements until you receive the year-end statement. Keep year-end statements with tax documents.

Paycheck stubs: Keep for a year until you get your year-end W-2. If everything is correct, shred the paycheck stubs.

Medical records: Save for seven years with tax documents. However, it seems I'm occasionally wanting to remember when something happened and have had to go back through past years' documents. What I should have done years ago is keep track of illnesses, surgeries, and minor procedures in a document of some kind. If this idea appeals to you, consider using a computer spreadsheet, record-keeping journals, or just buy a spiral notebook.

Home records: Keep all purchase and sale documents. Keep all home improvement expenses. Keep expenses related to selling your house. When you sell your house, you'll want these documents for tax purposes.

Automobile expenses: Keep all purchase documents and major repair receipts in case you sell the car. You'll want to pass these along to the new owner.

Vital Records

There are always documents you want to store in a secure, fireproof location. This list can change based on your individual situation. Experts generally agree on storing the following:

- Birth certificate(s)
- Will(s)
- Marriage certificate(s)
- Adoption certificate(s)
- Passport(s)
- Social security card(s)

Miscellaneous Paper Tips

Maybe you've got a handle on the "important" papers in your life, but the rest is weighing you down. Here are some tips for common paper issues.

Special Cards, Papers, and Letters

If you're like me, you love to keep birthday cards, a love note from your spouse, or a drawing from a child. Those items hold precious memories for me, such as the self-portrait my eldest son did in kindergarten—it was a rainbow.

Instead of tossing them in a big plastic tub, create some simple organization. An uncomplicated way to start is with a three-ring binder filled with acid-free page protectors. Just date the item, slip it into a page protector, and you're done.

To save my children's birthday cards, I put them in gallon zip-top plastic bags. These bags are stored in memory boxes in each child's room. I also tuck the guest list and a list of gifts received into the bag, along with a description of the party.

Phone Numbers, Addresses, and Passwords

Eliminate little pieces of paper! Let this be your organizing theme. A tool that works for me is a Rolodex-type address box. That's the kind with the removable cards. My advice is to transfer every name, address, and phone number to a Rolodex card. The beauty of this system is you can discard numbers you no longer need without messing up an address book. A Rolodex can also be used to store low- to medium-risk website passwords and account numbers. However, for high-risk accounts, use a different password and store it in a different place.

Magazines

I love my magazines. It's no surprise, given I'm a magazine editor by profession. If you'd like to check it out, please visit www.Proverbs31.org and click on "P31 Woman Magazine" for more information. My other favorites are *Victoria*, *Romantic Homes*, *Southern Living*, *Home Companion* (so sad that's not around anymore), and anything to do with food.

I look through each magazine multiple times, then enjoy seeing them fanned out on my coffee table. They are idea festivals for my mind! It's painful to part with them, as they become like friends.

However, having a plan makes it much easier to manage my magazines. Here are some suggestions:

- Display the current month only.
- If you haven't read the current issues, store them in a basket, in the order you need to read them.
- Hang a tote bag by the front door and put items you want to read in it. Take the bag with you when you know you'll have waiting time.

Once you've read a magazine, have a plan for the rest of its life. It's good stewardship to share magazines, especially if you have friends who can't afford to purchase them. Here are some ways to share the love:

- Donate to elementary schools for art projects.

- Donate to the library.
- Take to family functions and give away.
- Give to friends.
- Take to a church or community meeting and give away.

Where my plan falls apart is when I want to clip and save an article or idea. Then what? Each magazine contains organizing tips, decorating ideas, party themes, and places I'd like to visit. What do I do with those?

To save them, I created an "Idea Book" for about five dollars. It's simply a two-inch binder with a plastic sleeve on the front for a cover. Using Microsoft Publisher, I created a cover with images of my favorite magazines. I also bought some page protectors and a fresh glue stick. Tabbed dividers help sort ideas. Sections in my book include:

- Organization ideas
- Party decorations
- Recipes
- Gift ideas
- Decorating ideas

Menus and Museum Schedules

Have you ever picked up a museum brochure or a takeout menu and wondered where to put it? Consider creating your own "Family Fun Book." Another three-ring binder with tabbed inserts is all you need. Create different sections depending on your family's interests. As you collect information, put it in plastic page protectors or use a three-hole punch. Here are potential categories:

- Restaurant menus
- Party ideas
- Museum or activity brochures
- Movies you want to see or rent
- Ideas for day trips
- Vacation ideas

Reducing Paper for Good

Instead of just managing the paper clutter in your home or office, consider reducing it. Take a stack of paper, reviewing each item. Which newsletters, catalogs, or reports don't you need? Which magazines do you forget to read? Make a master list of whom to contact, then either shred or recycle the original pieces. Then, go through the process of either canceling your subscriptions or requesting a digital option. Here are other options for reducing paper for good.

Sign Up for Online Statements

Paying bills and reviewing statements online saves paper and time. This is an ecologically sound and secure way to reduce the amount of paper in the home. To keep up with the payments, I've used several options:

- **Automatic withdrawals**—These are preapproved by me to come out of my checking account on a certain day.
- **Tickler system**—I organize my paper bills in one spot, ordered chronologically by the due date. For bills I pay online but that aren't automatically withdrawn, I used to write the due date on an index card and rotate it along with the paper bills.
- **Outlook calendar**—Currently, I enter the dates on my Outlook calendar. I've set it up to remind me when to pay. It's synced with my phone, so I get the reminders two different ways.

Stop Credit Card Offers

The credit bureaus offer a toll-free number that enables you to "opt out" of having preapproved credit offers sent for five years. Call 1-888-5-OPTOUT (567-8688) or visit www.optoutprescreen.com for more information. When you call, you'll be asked for personal information, including your home telephone number, name, and social security number.

The information you provide is confidential and only used to process your request to opt out of receiving prescreened offers of credit.

Stop Direct-Marketing Mail

While the above-mentioned option is free, there is a service that charges one dollar to have your name removed from a variety of direct mail lists. The Direct Marketing Association (DMA) offers a mail preference service that allows you to choose which type of mail to stop for a period of five years:

- Credit offers
- Catalogs
- Magazine offers (this includes subscription offers, newsletters, periodicals, and other promotional mailings)
- Other mail offers (this includes donation requests, bank offers, retail promotions, and more)

When you register with this service, they put your name on a "delete" file and make it available to direct-mail marketers. Some organizations do not use the DMA's mail preference service, so it's not a perfect system. But most direct marketers are interested in maintaining positive customer service, and they will check this list. To register with DMA's mail preference service, go to www.dmachoice.org.

Scan and Store Electronically

Another option is to scan older documents if you still want to reference them, then keep them electronically, with a backup copy somewhere. Your backup could include a CD, flash drive, external hard drive, or remote hard drive. After my hard drive crashed, I signed up for www.carbonite.com. There's an annual fee, but it's worth the peace of mind. It backs up everything on my hard drive hourly, and I can access it from any computer with an Internet connection.

Identify theft is a serious problem. Many shy away from using online services for this reason. My advice is to educate yourself about the risks and benefits. Become an expert in safe Internet practices, and your confidence will increase as you make decisions based on fact, not fear.

Chapter Fourteen

Taming Technology

I have a love-hate relationship with my computer and cell phone. Well, actually, I just love them. What I hate is confessing my slight addiction to technology. And by "slight," I mean severe.

Being an editor and writer means using technology is a requirement of my job. So when I read advice telling me to limit consumption of technology, I discard it. It's like trying to lose weight. Not eating isn't an option, just as not using my computer isn't. However, I can incorporate healthy and smart practices into my day. Also, when I overindulge in food, I balance it out with restraint at other times or an increase in exercise. The same principles can be applied to my relationship with technology.

Actually, instead of weaning myself from technology, I'm investing time and money in educating myself on it. Especially since it's how I'll connect with other generations. I want to work smarter and consider how technology can assist, not hinder, my mission in life. You see, I'm passionate about reaching out to others in the name of Christ, and for me, that means staying current.

There's always the potential for distraction with any technology. Gadgets can waste an inordinate amount of time. The challenge is taming technology so it doesn't run our days. Keeping it in its place as a tool, not a temptation, takes work. Yet its potential for keeping us on track and efficient is worth the effort.

In this chapter, I'll look at the liabilities of technology multitasking, offer suggestions to bring greater focus to work, and provide tips for managing this indispensable part of our world. I'll start the chapter with some interesting information debunking the idea that multitasking makes us more efficient.

More Brain Downtime Is Needed

Researchers are discovering that a constant diet of technology changes the wiring in the brain—and not in a good way. Apparently, texting while surfing the Internet, while updating your status on Facebook, in between tweeting your peeps is making it harder and harder to focus. Really? What a surprise.

Most of the research is done on teenagers and twentysomethings who have grown up with a phone on their hip and a computer on their desk. Those generations are multitasking animals. Sadly, the research shows they also have trouble sustaining focus because of it. Yet, it's not an exclusive problem. As older adults increasingly use technology to multitask, the same problem happens to us. If you've worried you have an attention disorder, it might just be that your brain isn't designed for multitasking.

The *New York Times* featured an article titled "Growing Up Digital, Wired for Distraction" by Matt Richtel. Richtel reports, "The lure of these technologies, while it affects adults too, is particularly powerful for young people. The risk, they say, is that developing brains can become more easily habituated than adult brains to constantly switching tasks—and less able to sustain attention."[1]

The problem is that increased exposure to electronic stimuli keeps the brain active even when not in front of a screen, thereby decreasing the brain's ability to rest. The constant state of stimulation isn't healthy for anyone. Our brains need rest like our bodies need sleep.

Could an inability to sustain focus be hindering your ability to bring order and balance into your life? If so, then it's time to address this half-life of electronic mental stimulation, by balancing it with times of mental rest. We need less consumption of technology and more unplugged activities, like reading and getting in to nature. Even sitting with a cup of tea staring at the rain can help.

Here's the takeaway for us: Even though it may seem like you are saving time by multitasking, you're not as efficient or effective as you might think.

The Myth of Multitasking

Given the research mentioned above, the bragging should cease immediately regarding multitasking. No longer should we proudly flaunt our ability to juggle a variety of tasks—especially those concerning technology. It seems being a multitasker damages one's ability to turn off distractions at critical times. In other words, when we need to bring full focus and energy to the task at hand, we can't. Which might explain why projects take longer, tasks are harder to break down, and getting through piles of paper is mentally exhausting.

Clifford Nass, a Stanford University cognitive scientist, wanted to know the impact of multitasking on an individual's ability to focus. In a study published in 2009 in the *Proceedings of the National Academy of Sciences*, Nass and Stanford psychologists Anthony Wagner and Eyal Ophir surveyed 262 students on their media consumption habits. Of those students, the group who multitasked the most and another who multitasked least took two computer-based tests.[2]

In every test, students who spent *less time* simultaneously reading e-mail, surfing the web, talking on the phone, and watching TV performed best.

Another study showed that only two and a half percent of people are actually super-multitaskers.[3] These select few can switch from task to task with ease. Interestingly, most people think they are in that two and a half percent. I took a focus test online and thought I aced it when I saw how high my results were. Looking closer, it was apparent I was off the charts the wrong direction.

The reality is most of us aren't as productive as we think when there are multiple streams of information and interruptions entering our psyche. It's much safer to assume we are in the majority and function *less* effectively while multitasking. If we want to do our best work, we need a return to *monotasking*, doing one thing at a time.

The good news is we can learn concentration. Monotasking helps, and it is easy to start practicing. You don't have to go into a soundproof booth. Start by turning off the television, iPod, or CD and focusing on one task. Then, once you've got that down, turn off the phone, shut down your e-mail program, and disconnect from instant messaging. Practice bringing your straying attention back to the project.

Although you may not immediately see the benefits of renewed focus, over time you'll experience greater control over your thoughts. David Allen, author of *Ready for Anything*, says this about productivity, "At any moment, giving full attention to the one thing at hand is a hallmark of high performance."[4]

As we seek to return to a place of order and peace in our lives, we must be able to process a problem from beginning to end with clarity and focus. Researchers will continue to study the connection between technology use and focus, but for now, using it with limits and wisdom is the best approach.

For the rest of the chapter, I've assembled some tips on managing technology. Any time I write on technology, I know it will be outdated soon. Hopefully you'll find broad enough tips to apply now and in the future.

Digital Planning

Having the right planner is essential for staying organized in our busy lives. The hallmark of a successful planner is its ability to capture all the information you need in one place. With hundreds of options on the market, you may have to try a few before settling on one that works. But don't feel pressured to get a digital planner. A paper calendar might work well for you. My sister, a grade school teacher, is quite efficient with her pocket-sized, two-year calendar.

However, my eighty-four-year-old mother might need an electronic planner. She oversees an important church committee on a state level. She's attending meetings and doing some travelling. She often needs to keep more information than just a starting time. She may need to have addresses, names, and phone numbers handy, or remind herself of a document that she needs. A digital planner offers the flexibility she needs.

As demands on your life change, consider changing your planner. Remember, what worked years ago may not work today. Here are some principles for picking the right planner.

Be clear on what you need to record. Make a list of elements that would help you be more effective. Then research planners with those components. Here are some helpful sections:

Appointments
To-do lists
Project lists
Prayer lists
Meeting notes
Grocery lists
Pending

Consider options for traditional and electronic planners. The best place to find options for electronic planners is the Internet. Search using the keywords "digital planners" or "electronic organizers" or any combination of those words. There are also online programs to help manage tasks. Some websites to start your search include:

- Remember the Milk (www.rememberthemilk.com)
- Amy Napp's Family Organizer (www.thefamilyorganizer. com)
- A Life Well Lived (www.christiandayplanners.org)

- David Allen, Getting Things Done system
  (www.davidco.com)
- Franklin Covey (www.store.franklinplanner.com)
- My Life Organized (www.mylifeorganized.net)

Combine work and home schedules. Integrating work and home allows you to review your evening plans while still at work and vice versa. It's not marrying both—it's connecting both. It's unrealistic to think any of us can keep these completely separate. Being a realist by nature, I find it's more logical to figure out how to make them work together.

Sync digital calendar with phone. Years ago, I wanted a BlackBerry because I liked the name. Now that I have one, I realize it's got more benefits than a cute name. I use Outlook and sync it on my BlackBerry and have instant access to my calendar, notes for appointments, contact list, and more.

My friend Sarah Martin shared a great tip about making the most of her digital calendar. Sarah said, "If someone has an event or need for prayer at a specific time, I create an appointment on my calendar for that prayer need and then set the reminder from that screen. I set an alert on my phone to remind me to pray. I usually send my friend a note (text or e-mail) to tell them I prayed or type out the prayer for them. I'm all about phone calls and face to face time, but that's not always possible at the moment the prayer is needed." Sarah's idea shows how technology can be an effective tool for ministry and saving time.

Make the most of all product features. My MO for most technology has been to learn the least amount needed to get by. But no more. Now, I force myself to learn all of the features and shortcuts of my electronic devices. I've learned something amazing: the designers are smarter than I am.

They've actually tucked all kinds of productivity supports tips into these devices. So get all the worth of your money and effort, and learn all you can.

Texting

I've got a few friends that text. We've discovered it's an efficient way to communicate certain things. Mind you, not everything can be communicated this way. Some messages are too long or complicated for a text. However, if you have a quick message to get to a friend, consider texting. Its benefits include:

- They can read it when they have time.
- It takes less time than a phone call.
- You can tell your kids you love them without embarrassing them.

My friend Melissa texts a Bible verse to her children every day. That's a creative way to use texting.

Managing Your Computer

Regularly hire someone to come in and clean up your hard drive. Once a year, I bring in an expert to make sure my computer is streamlined, cleaned up, and loaded with the latest products to keep it running smoothly. This bit of maintenance saves me hours of time over a year in slow processing or, worse, lost documents.

Also, invest in a remote backup for your hard drive. I use Carbonite online backup. Although there's an annual fee, it's a worthwhile investment in my work and gives me peace of mind.

The Internet

The Internet not only saves me time, but I get the most up-to-date information on current topics. I can also click on any link that promises cute pictures of animals. And it makes me think about a YouTube video I once saw with a husky saying "I love you." *I simply must watch that one more time—it's only sixty seconds. My husky yodels, too, but why can't I train her to walk—not run?* Then I start surfing for dog training websites, husky websites, Dog Whisperer websites . . . I wonder if he's done a segment on making huskies walk . . . and so it goes.

I don't have ADD, but you'd think I did at times. It takes discipline, pure and simple, to stay focused on the Internet. Here are some tips to help:

- Bookmark favorite sites—you'll spend less time searching.
- Block pop-up ads.
- Invest in a good filter. (We use Bsecure Online.)
- Create folders for favorite sites. I've got folders for recipes, publishers, school sites, etc.
- Create subfolders.
- Refuse to click on interesting links.

Managing E-mail

For most people in my generation, e-mail is still our key method of business communication. My teenagers don't have an e-mail account, and their generation won't be quite as dependent on it as we have been. But for now, my business and ministry life center on e-mail. Honestly, it overwhelms me at times. But I've learned a few techniques that help me stay in control. While I may not always get my inbox to zero every day, I do keep it manageable. (Except after vacations. Somehow, I take twice as long as my vacation to catch up).

Checking E-mail

Most experts agree that e-mail can be an addiction. If you find yourself constantly checking your inbox during meals or in the middle of the night, you might need an intervention. Hopefully, it's not that bad. The tips for keeping it under control are quite simple . . . if you are willing to follow them.

The first step to controlling e-mail is to schedule when you review them. Allow yourself time in your day to read and respond to them. This may mean once, twice, or three times a day. By scheduling enough time to review e-mails, you can handle them in that sitting and be done with them. However, if you receive them throughout the day, you'll either read them and think you responded, or stop your current focus and get off track.

Let your co-workers and friends know your schedule for checking e-mail. If you are consistent in not responding immediately, they might just learn to solve their own problems.

Creating Folders

Creating e-mail file folders is a great way to organize information. Since most of us use Outlook, I can walk you through the process. There are several ways to create a folder. For example, let's say you want to put all your e-mails about your summer vacation plans in one place. The easiest way to do it is to right-click on the e-mail you want to store. Then, click on "move to folder" at the bottom. If you need to create a new folder, then click on "new," title the folder, and click "OK." The e-mail automatically moves to the new folder. For those of us who use another email system, instructions for creating new folders should be easy to locate once you are logged-in.

An important tip is to make fewer general folders and more subfolders. If you have too many folders, you'll lose things. Example: Create one "Vacation" folder and then a subfolder for each year, and then individual folders for each trip.

Some of my general folders include: Family (includes subfolders for each child, vacations, etc.), Articles to review, Organization newsletters, and She Speaks (an annual conference). I tuck e-mails in these folders with important correspondence.

Here are a few suggestions for helpful folders you might create:

- Pending
- Delegated
- To read
- To review

Regularly purge your e-mail folders. You can crash your system by storing too many.

Creating Filters

Once you've created folders, you can create rules sending incoming e-mails directly to these folders. You can create a rule based on any number of criteria: who the e-mail is from (like your mom), keywords in the subject line, distribution lists, and more. These filters will start the organizational work for you and store e-mails by theme. I have filters in place for Facebook and blog comments, my writer's group, and a few more.

Using Automated Response

Many people use an automatic response when they will be out of the office. This tool can also be used to manage how you respond to your e-mails. If your company allows, set up an automated response letting people know when you check your e-mails. Then, set up specific times during the day to do so.

Managing Facebook

I opened a Facebook account out of guilt. Within minutes, I somehow invited everyone I'd ever e-mailed, or who had e-mailed me, to be my friend. The first clue was when people I didn't know were "accepting" my friend request. The second clue was when the moderator of an online writers' group (with a thousand members) told me it was "illegal" to use the group list in that way. Gulp. It was an embarrassing way to start my Facebook experience.

I have two pieces of advice: 1) Don't do anything out of perceived obligation (including Twitter, LinkedIn, Myspace, etc.); and 2) learn all you can beforehand. Here are some other general tips for managing Facebook or other social networks.

Know your purpose. Without a clear purpose, you'll be quickly overwhelmed and stressed. If you know you want to make business connections, then be clear about that. If you only want to connect with close friends and family, that's fine, too.

Create private and public profiles. Don't mix personal information and business. Michael Hyatt, CEO of Thomas Nelson, went through his experience with this in a public way. He eventually closed down one site and opened an Official Page and a Personal Page—which was limited to people he actually knew. Research the options for pages on Facebook.

Be selective in your friends. Don't do anything out of guilt. You will regret it later—especially if you need to unfriend someone.

Make your status updates meaningful. Please don't tell me you are going to bed. Refer back to your purpose when questioning what to post.

Use Facebook as a pathway to human connection. Online relationships are much easier than real ones. Make sure Facebook doesn't replace face-to-face relationships.

Delete and start fresh. If you have too many "friends" you don't know, delete your account and start a new one.

A Simple Grid

The Amish have a process called "selective modernization." When something new reaches into their community, they give serious consideration to whether it's a good fit for their chosen lifestyle. They weigh its long-term effects against possible benefits. They consider if the new equipment or technology draws them closer to God or further away. They question how it will affect the family, the home, and the community.

The Amish have a saying: *Once drawn, lines are hard to erase*. Before adding a new piece of technology to our lives, perhaps we could put it through the same evaluation process. Proverbs 14:1 says, "The wise woman builds her house, but with her own hands the foolish one tears hers down." Each decision we make is a building block in our homes and lives. Take your time, pray, and seek wise counsel before crossing any technological line you can't erase gracefully.

. . . .

Chapter Fifteen

Keeping the Kitchen the Heart of the Home

. . . . ❧ . . . .

Robbie was getting ready for a wrestling tournament and wanted breakfast. Complex carbohydrates are wise before an athletic event, so we prepared oatmeal with sliced bananas, toast, and a berry smoothie. The table was set with a placemat, napkin, and spoon. I warmed some milk for his oatmeal, and he poured it into the steaming bowl. Grabbing my coffee, I joined him at the table.

He ate a spoonful of oatmeal and sipped his smoothie. He grinned, took another bite, and said, "I feel like I'm in a country kitchen."

I knew what he meant. Even though our suburban home is far from any "country," that simple statement spoke a longing for simplicity, a slower pace, and the nurture of family. His teenage body is pulling a little boy out of childhood and into the world of independence, but his heart is planted firmly at home, in his mother's kitchen.

A contented smile settled on me all morning, as I thought about how many of life's blessings happen in my kitchen. This room unites the values I hold dear: home, family, and community. This is why keeping it organized and clutter-free is a top priority for me. It's not so I can boast of my alphabetized spices or labeled storage containers. An organized kitchen helps me focus on what's important, instead of being mentally drained by a mess.

My kitchen also needs the most work to stay organized. As I write this book, all five of my children live at home, plus my husband and I both work here. My front door should be a big hotel revolving door with the flow of people in and out all day. Because my office space is adjacent to the kitchen, I get to hug and kiss a lot of my favorite people as they make their way through the house. But there's also a problem with this many people.

As my pride-and-joys move through the house, personal property gets set down in the most convenient spot . . . convenient to them, that is. This normally means a kitchen counter. Without ongoing attention, my kitchen counters are like a volcano, erupting and overflowing.

Here's the problem with a disorganized kitchen. When there's no room to work, I'm discouraged from starting anything. Instead of making an affordable and healthy dinner, I am tempted to pick up something fast. Instead of being creative in the kitchen, I choose something simple. It just takes too much mental energy for me to overcome clutter.

Not only does clutter drain energy from me, but there is no room for anything beautiful when there's stuff all over my counters. It's hard to appreciate a bouquet of roses from my garden if it's set on bills, report cards, and dirty dishes.

So, in order to bring in more beauty, peace, and order, I have declared a war on clutter—on my counters and in my cabinets and pantry. Here's a step-by-step approach to organizing your kitchen.

Step One: Reclaim the Kitchen for Your Desired Purpose

What's your vision for your kitchen? Is it a haven for yourself and family? A blank canvas for your inner chef? A hospitality center for guests? Maybe all three? Allow yourself to envision your ideal purpose for your kitchen.

That exercise is more than just daydreaming. Establishing or re-establishing the purpose of your kitchen will help you clarify guidelines for what stays and what goes. In my experience, too much gets placed by default in the kitchen. Here's what should not be stored on kitchen counters, and some alternate ideas:

Keys	Hang a decorative key rack by the front door.
Wallets	Place a rattan box with a lid by the front door.
Sunglasses	Ditto
Backpacks	Freestanding coat rack
Library books	Basket in the living room
Papers to sign	One pretty inbox
Misc. notes	Decorative message board near phone or in laundry room

Take some time to think through where something should logically and realistically be stored. If your husband is not going to walk to the bedroom to put his cell phone on the dresser, then be creative and make it easy for him to place it somewhere that is not your kitchen counter. It isn't worth any conflict, so work around it.

Once your family has a place for their important items, they just need gentle training until it's a habit.

Step Two: Eliminate Excess Kitchen Accoutrements

My first kitchen was always organized because there wasn't much there. Less is definitely easier. As we established ourselves over the years, we accumulated many cooking and serving pieces.

You might get tired of hearing this piece of advice, but there is no point in shifting unwanted or unused stuff from a cabinet to a pantry and back again. Keep your kitchen slim and trim by finding a better home for those fondue pots and pink serving bowls that don't match your red dishes.

My goal is also to store most if not all kitchen appliances out of sight. Clean and clear kitchen counters refresh and provide a clean palette for creativity. It's going to get worse before it gets better, because I want you to identify cabinets or pantry shelves that need attention and remove every item, placing them on the counters. Wash shelves and allow to dry. Then . . .

1. Ruthlessly dispose of:

- Storage containers without lids.
- Broken appliances. (It will likely cost more to fix than replace most items these days.)
- Chipped glass or ceramic items.

2. Donate, or set aside for a garage sale, items in good shape that you never use. Be honest with yourself. Your heart might long for the smell of homemade bread wafting from your kitchen. But if the closest you get to homemade bread is the grocery store, you might want to sell the bread maker. Same goes for the rice maker, vegetable dehydrator, and juicer. (That sales guy at the fair is good!) And that turkey fryer that seemed like such a good idea when your brother-in-law used one . . . yeah . . . it's probably time for that to go, too.

I've been married twenty-six years and still have a serving bowl we received as a gift. At one time, I wanted everything pink! Now, it's time for that bowl to find another home. I'm also not likely to polish silver, and I have given away beautiful pieces to someone who will take better care of them.

If storage allows, keep items to give to your children when they set up their own homes. It's a great way to keep meaningful gifts in the family and help your kids establish independence.

3. Think seriously about replacing:

- Mismatched glasses and plates. Glasses in a cylinder shape take up less space.
- Round storage containers. Square or rectangle ones also conserve space.

4. Store seldom-used appliances elsewhere. If kitchen space is limited, consider storing larger items outside your kitchen. If you are holding

out hope that you will start to use your waffle iron, then consider a shelf in an outside storage cabinet, extra bedroom, or linen closet. I have a shelf in my garage for larger items I don't often use.

Another option is to purchase extra kitchen storage, like a freestanding pantry or rolling island. Consider buying something with doors to reduce visual clutter.

Step Three: Add Space-Saving Equipment

While assessing the reorganization of your kitchen, consider whether space-saving equipment would help. There are many products available, most at affordable rates, to help make the most of the space you have. If you don't know what's available, visit www.containerstore.com or www. organize.com for great ideas. Here are some popular ideas:

- Stacking shelves for cabinets
- Can organizers
- Tiered organizers for smaller items
- Pull-out shelves for deeper cabinets
- Built-in spice racks
- Drawer dividers

Step Four: Store Items Near Point of Use

When replacing items, store them near their final point of use. Baking and cooking items go near the oven and stove. Dishes belong near the dishwasher or sink.

Step Five: Organize Food

As you look at kitchen organization, consider two other benefits.

Eating healthier. As a nation, we eat too much processed food. I get that. It's much easier to make boxed scalloped potatoes and snack on crackers or chips. Spending time in people's kitchens tells me we might have more than an organization problem.

As you tackle the foods stored in your kitchen, consider reducing processed and packaged items and replacing them with foods in their natural state. Not only will this help with organization by reducing boxes, but you'll also eat healthier. In Chapter Sixteen, I cover menu planning, which should help if you desire to move in this direction.

Saving money. Staying organized also saves money because you can avoid purchasing duplicate items. When your pantry and cabinets are streamlined, you'll see at a glance what you need. No one needs four containers of pumpkin pie spice or five jars of pickle relish taking up valuable space.

Once cabinets are in order, it's time to turn to food. Here are more step-by-step directions on addressing food storage.

Refrigerator/Freezer

Keeping our refrigerators and freezers organized not only helps avoid waste but sets the stage for healthier eating. Consider these tips:

- Throw away anything with mold or that is beyond its expiration date. It's not good stewardship if someone gets sick, or you use something questionable in a recipe and have to discard the entire dish.
- Combine like items when safe (as with condiments).
- Eat leftovers. Create a menu for the following week where you intentionally use leftovers. Use the oldest first.
- Use partially empty items or older frozen items by creating menus around them.
- Wash the inside and outside of your refrigerator with warm, soapy water. Then create a beautiful display on the top with plants, baskets, or other decorative items. You'll take more pride in the contents that way.

I love to try new recipes, and I don't mind purchasing a unique seasoning or condiment once in awhile. The problem is that I might use half the jar, then it gets stuck in the fridge. Every once in awhile, I make a list of those items and incorporate them into the week's menu.

Recently, my refrigerator had partially full containers of mango chutney, spaghetti sauce, frosting, capers, and bruschetta mixture. My menu that week included chicken Parmesan, fish with a tomato-caper sauce, and bruschetta appetizers for a potluck.

Pantry/Cupboards

My pantry needs constant upkeep. But every once it awhile it needs more than simple rearranging. When it's time for an overhaul, here are some steps I take:

- Remove all items. Thoroughly clean the shelves and allow to dry.
- Check expiration dates and discard items far past the safe date. The date on most canned or bottled food is the ideal use date. Normally, there is healthy use past that date. But to be safe, don't wait more than a few months.
- Make a list of items that are close to the expiration date, and incorporate them into your menus in the coming weeks.
- Set aside fresh items to donate to a food bank, especially if you have an abundance.
- Combine like items that have a similar expiration date. This would apply to items such as cereals, crackers, or dry mixes.
- Sort food items into logical groupings as you replace them. Place loose items in baskets or bins.

Step Six: Maintain Order

Once you've reclaimed your kitchen, small daily habits can keep it that way. Old habits are hard to break, but the benefits of creativity, good stewardship, increased health, and a restful place for family gatherings will motivate you. Here are a few tips I use to maintain order in my kitchen.

Clean and replace as I cook. It takes work to make this a habit, but once it's ingrained, it will change your kitchen forever. As I use an item in cooking, I immediately replace it. Sometimes, I'll put up two or three items at once, but the principle is the same: Don't wait until you are done to start cleaning up. This may mean a few extra trips to the fridge, but I avoid feeling overwhelmed and sitting down to watch TV instead of cleaning up.

Clean the kitchen before bed. I love waking up to clean counters!

Keep the stovetop and sink clean. FlyLady (Marla Cilley) says keeping your sink clean is the first step to organizing your kitchen. "That shiny sink is contagious to the rest of the kitchen; just like your happiness and sadness is infectious to your family."[1]

Train family members in cooking and cleaning. If you've got extra bodies in your home, you've got help.

General Kitchen Tips

1. Invest in a few really good kitchen items, and you'll find you need less. Having several high-quality knives, and keeping them sharp, reduces the need for several kitchen appliances.
2. Don't use an electric can opener. If you lose electricity, you want to be able to open a can. Plus, it's one less appliance to store. And you burn five calories instead of one. I think.
3. Once your counters are clean, create some lovely vignettes: a coffee center, a bouquet of fresh flowers, a candle, and a bowl of candy. Decorative placemats can serve as the base.
4. Put a basket or box (make it attractive) near the kitchen for items that need to find their rightful homes elsewhere.
5. Create a transition center for items that need to be taken out of the house. Place by the main exit door.

6. Keep a permanent marker in the kitchen to mark the date food is placed in the freezer. Use most frozen items within three to six months. Some meat can last nine months.

Chapter Sixteen

. . . .

Meal Planning for Health and Sanity

. . . . ❧ . . . .

America has a renewed love affair with food—especially the home-cooked kind. More folks than ever know how to puree, sauté, and flambé. The Food Network stars are familiar friends at my house. All I have to say is, "This is a 'Paula' recipe," and my family knows it will have butter and sour cream in it somehow. I'll admit I'm a foodie.

In spite of my love for all things kitchen-related, meal planning and preparation can derail both my schedule and emotions. When my own lack of planning puts me behind, an innocent question of "What's there to eat?" sets me at all kinds of odds. This required fuel for daily living has the power to take my focus off priorities, cause me to overspend, and steal my time.

This isn't a new issue. Jesus told his disciples not to worry about what they would eat or drink in Matthew 6:25 because it was a problem for them. Not because Jesus didn't want them eating, but because even for those first followers of Jesus, food was taking the wrong place in their hearts.

Is it possible we have elevated food above the position God intended? I believe he wants us to enjoy food—otherwise, we wouldn't have pizza and brownies. But it was never meant to dominate our days and checkbooks with overindulgence and unnecessary time and money spent running to the store or through fast-food establishments.

The answer to managing food correctly is planning. Thirty minutes a week of planning could save hundreds of dollars a month and countless little frustrations. By simply planning meals, families would:

- Be healthier.
- Be more organized.
- Have more peace at home.
- Spend more time together.
- Save money.
- Minister to other families in need.
- Extend hospitality.

With a plan, food takes its proper place in our households—and that's a healthy necessity and an enjoyable part of the day spent with those important to us.

So many women I meet find this part of their schedule to be an overwhelming burden. They don't like to cook, and they like grocery shopping even less. When faced with those two requirements of meal planning, takeout food and a restaurant are appealing alternatives. But consider for a moment the amount of time and money wasted on those two options. Maybe even more important than those two considerations are the health benefits of eating at home.

When you can control your ingredients and portion sizes, you are on your way to a healthier lifestyle. When I go out to eat, vegetables are usually the last thing I worry about. Unless, of course, it's a salad . . . smothered in blue cheese dressing and a potato topped with chives. Does that count as a vegetable? You get my point. When I plan my menu, I work in the right amount of fruits, vegetables, dairy, starch, and protein.

Are there organizational benefits to a healthy lifestyle? Absolutely! When you have increased energy and health, you are better able to manage the requirements of your day. Studies show that eating protein in the morning gives you sustained energy throughout the day and increased mental alertness.

Judith Wurtman, PhD, director of a women's health program at the MIT Clinical Research Center in Boston says two brain chemicals govern mental alertness: epinephrine and dopamine, which are made from an amino acid called tyrosine—which comes from protein! We don't need that much of it, just a couple of ounces. Wurtman, quoted in "Eat to Boost Mental Alertness" states, "If you consume protein before a task, you can make sure whatever brainpower you, or your child, had going in is still there at the end of the task. Carbs do not really have an effect on mental alertness."[1]

Brain Food

Low fat cottage cheese
Yogurt
Scrambled eggs, with both the yolks and whites
Veggie burgers
Peanut butter
Whole-grain toast

Hot and cold cereal, English muffins (as long as you eat them along with protein)

Source: www.medicinenet.com

Unfortunately, many of us grab the easiest thing in the morning—cereal, toast, or a bagel —and then wonder why we don't have any energy by 10 a.m. Not only are we experiencing a carbohydrate mid-morning crash, for which we head for caffeine and another crash in a few hours, but we

have denied ourselves the nutrients our bodies and minds need to function at their best.

Have I convinced you yet that planning meals is an all-around good
thing? I hope so. Now that I've got you thrilled about this idea, let's see
how to incorporate it into your already busy life.

Steps of Menu Planning

Before you start, you'll need a few things:

- Your week's schedule, including evening events
- Grocery store ads
- Pad of paper and pen
- Recipe books or access to the Internet

While some people like to plan for a month at a time, I think a week is
more manageable. That way I can usually make one trip to the store, purchasing a variety of fresh and packaged items that will last for seven days.
For me, weekends are a good time to plan, and I focus on dinner primarily
because that's where we have the most variety in our day.

Your schedule is your starting place. By looking at each day, you'll
identify which nights you have time to cook and which nights you'll need
to depend on the slow cooker or something precooked (either by you or
the store). You'll also know which nights you don't need to cook, based
on a special event, or which nights might work for leftovers.

Step One—Be Hungry

Make sure you are hungry. This is a must. Do not sit down after lunch or
dinner to plan your menu. You will be full and nothing will sound good.
The hungrier you are, the better. As an aside, you should *not* go to the
grocery store hungry, or you'll end up with chocolate-covered graham
crackers and nacho chips, neither of which is brain food. Please trust that
I know of which I write. But when you make your weekly menu hungry,
even the most "boring" recipe sounds wonderful. You might even try
brussels sprouts or eggplant.

Step Two—Identify Main Ingredients

Create a list of the main ingredients you will use that week. The first place to start is in your refrigerator or freezer. If you've got something that needs to be used up before it goes bad, include it in your list.

Another option is to read through the grocery store ads for specials. I write this assuming most readers are looking to save money. If you are one of the few who doesn't worry about this, then looking through the ads will give you ideas.

As you look through the ads, make a list of items that are on sale and could be the basis of a meal. For example, in my ads this week, here are some of the great buys:

- pork chops
- shredded cheese
- tilapia
- eggs
- boneless, skinless chicken breasts
- bratwurst

Immediately, I can think of the foundations for some yummy meals.

- Pork chops in the slow cooker with sauerkraut and apples
- Quiche with ham and cheese
- Grilled tilapia with lemon pepper seasoning
- Chicken enchiladas
- BBQ bratwurst sandwiches with peppers and onions

Most often I prepare my menu starting with the main ingredient, then I look for a recipe that includes that item. But that's not always the case. When I've got time, I go recipe hunting first. Either way works.

Step Three—Find Recipes for the Star of Your Meal

With your list of main course ingredients (hamburger, chicken, etc.), start looking through cookbooks, recipe cards, or Internet sites for ideas for the center of your meal. This would be the meatloaf, baked chicken, or chef salad.

If you don't own any cookbooks, check some out from the library. Grab two or three each time you go. If you aren't comfortable with reading recipes, then select a cookbook with lots of photos.

I'm a firm believer in buying cookbooks, too. If a new cookbook keeps me from going out to eat once, it has already paid for itself.

The Internet is a great place to find ideas. My favorite sites are www. shecooks.org, www.foodnetwork.com, www.cooks.com, and www.food. com. All of these sites allow you to search for recipes using an ingredient. These are just a few of my favorites. When I find a recipe or site I like, I bookmark it on my computer for easy access when it's time to cook.

Make sure you plan some meals using your slow cooker for busy days. There is nothing like coming home from a busy day at work to the smell of chili or soup simmering in your slow cooker. It can be especially helpful on a night when your family is coming and going at odd times.

It's very important that you record exactly where you found the recipe. It's embarrassing to think about the number of times I have been *certain* I would remember where I found a recipe, only to stand in the kitchen at 5 p.m. with no idea which cookbook or Internet site it's on.

Step Four—Pick Your Side Dishes

While it's nice to know you are having steak or chicken, you also need to plan what to eat alongside those main dishes in order to fulfill all your nutritional needs. Here's where you get to fill in your daily fruit and vegetable requirements.

As you plan your menu, make sure you add interesting sides. Normally, if my main dish is simple, I choose a side with some variety. For example, if I grill chicken, I might make scalloped potatoes to go with it. But if I'm serving a more complicated main dish like turkey tetrazzini, I would choose a simple vegetable like broccoli or green beans.

To make sure your family is getting their daily recommended intake of all the food groups, go to www.mypyramid.gov for the most recent government guidelines. Remember, these are just guidelines, because everyone is different. I've included sample amounts for women below.

Recommended Daily Intake
For women aged 20 to 50
Women under 30 should choose the higher number

Fruits: 1.5 to 2 cups
Vegetables: 2 to 2.5 cups
Grains: 6-ounce equivalent (half should be whole grains)
Dairy: 3 cups
Meat and beans: 5- to 5.5-ounce equivalent
Oils: 5 to 6 teaspoons

From www.mypyramid.gov
US Department of Agriculture

Step Five—Be Creative

One of the benefits of planning ahead is you can incorporate fun and creative items into your week. The possibilities are endless. I challenge myself to come up with at least one special item every few weeks, and I make it something I look forward to.

Here's one example. While normally we don't eat dessert, sometimes I'll plan a treat like bananas foster. This is easy to make, but it does take some planning. It starts with melted butter and brown sugar, into which sliced bananas are added. We adapt it slightly by leaving out the rum, and we spoon this caramel-like, banana-laden sauce over vanilla ice cream. We've done this at home and enjoyed a touch of the French Quarter.

For some out-of-the norm ideas, look at restaurant menus. If chefs can cook it in a restaurant, you can almost always make it at home. I love to order the French dip sandwich at a restaurant. I always thought it was too much trouble to cook a roast just for roast beef. Then I tried to make these sandwiches at home using deli roast beef, and they were delicious. The au jus can be made from a packet, and bakery rolls complete the recipe. Round out the meal with a coleslaw, and you've got an easy restaurant-style meal at home.

I've also discovered there are some great copycat recipes available. A popular one is the hash brown casserole served at Cracker Barrel. You can find some recipes free on the Internet or purchase cookbooks.

Other creative ideas include picking a theme, such as a Hawaiian luau or an Oktoberfest menu. Try going vegetarian or vegan.

Step Six—Plan Your Breakfast and Lunch

Since breakfast is important, we should also consider planning nutritious meals for the morning. My kids love yogurt, fruit, and granola parfaits, but the only way they get them is if I plan. To be honest, I don't put as much thought into breakfast and lunch as I do dinner. But I make sure we've got options that are healthy and easy to serve.

Having protein-rich foods easily available is especially important at breakfast. Hard-boiled eggs, precooked turkey sausage, and peanut butter spread on a whole-grain English muffin are simple ways to get a protein boost.

Mornings are a stressful time for most people, especially parents. I'll never forget the time two of my kids sat bickering at the breakfast table over who got to watch which television program. I grabbed the TV remote, pointed it at them, and tried to turn them off. They were pretty sure I'd lost it, and they were right.

From that day forward, the TV has been turned off in the morning, and we all experience less stress. Having a plan for breakfast has also helped.

Step Seven—Schedule Your Dinners

Once you've got your dinner items identified, then drop them into your schedule based on available time. For example, if you have a crazy busy night planned, with people coming and going, then a slow cooker recipe is perfect. Add a green salad in the fridge and a loaf of French bread, and dinner is served from 6 to 9 p.m.

If You Hate to Cook

Even with the best plan, I know some of you dear readers dread cooking more than any other task of the day. Here are some ideas for you:

- Get in a cooking co-op with friends. Join with two or three other friends whose families mirror yours in size. Meet once a month to plan your menus and assign days. Then you cook for your friends one night, and they take turns cooking for you.
- Cook more than one meal at a time. Just get it over with on one day of the week.
- Cook one item and have a plan for leftovers. (For example, cook a beef roast on Sunday, and use the shredded meat for tacos another day.)
- Make one-dish meals (aka casseroles). By putting everything in one dish, you eliminate a lot of cleanup and cooking.
- Incorporate some frozen dinners into your menu. I always have go-to meals in the freezer. When I shop at my local warehouse store, I find I can buy some meals cheaper than I can make them. They are a great way to ease the stress on some nights.

Putting Food in Its Right Place

Although this chapter considers the practical aspects of meal planning, the truth is that food is a beautiful gift from a loving heavenly Father. It's a delightful way to keep our bodies healthy, enjoy the flavors of the world around us, and connect with each other. Yet for many, instead of being a tool for a productive life, food becomes an idol or even a master of our time, finances, and thoughts.

By taking control of food and placing it in its rightful place in our lives, we are establishing habits and routines that free us to embrace all of God's design for this necessary ingredient of life. Not only does God intend for food to bring health, enjoyment, and connection, but I believe God also uses it to grow his church. We discover that eating meals together was an important part of early church growth in the book of Acts.

Acts 2 paints a simple picture of the early church. It describes a community of people devoted "to the apostles' teaching and to the fellowship, to the breaking of bread and to prayer" (Acts 2:42). Verse 46 says, "Every day they continued to meet together in the temple courts. They broke bread in their homes and ate together with glad and sincere hearts." Verse 47 wraps up that chapter with, "And the Lord added to their number daily those who were being saved."

God used food to bring people together so they could hear the life-changing message of the gospel, and he still does that today. By having a plan for food, we are able to enjoy a more relaxed and organized day, plus reach out in hospitality and ministry to those in need. And that is a very good thing.

. . . .

Chapter Seventeen

Beautiful Bedrooms
and Baths

. . . . ∽ . . . .

When we moved into our home, I devoted all resources to the main living areas, the playroom, and the children's bedrooms. Years later, I finally attended to the master bedroom. I took out the overstuffed bookshelves, moved a chest of drawers into the closet, replaced the bedspread, and added a comfortable reading chair. Less clutter and more intentionality transformed the room. Why did I wait so long?

Many women put the needs of others ahead of themselves. I wouldn't tell you to do anything else. But I will encourage you to prioritize your personal spaces. In this chapter, I'll address practical ways to bring order to your bedroom and bathroom.

More than making them functional, your private rooms, above all others, should be havens. They should be retreats from the world, places of rest and beauty. This doesn't mean perfectly decorated. It doesn't mean you can't work there, either. It does mean you create places in which you can recharge and de-stress.

Before starting to reorganize your bedroom or bath, cast a vision for each. Check out design books from the library, buy a decorating magazine, or visit HGTV's website. The purpose of this exploration isn't to create a list of "wants." It's to inspire you when you feel overwhelmed. Without spending any money, all of us can simplify and beautify what we already have. What touches of beauty would you like to see?

Touches of Beauty

A redecorating project isn't in the budget for most of us, but all of us can incorporate touches of beauty on a smaller scale. As you cast this vision for your private rooms, consider what vignettes of loveliness you can add. Here are some suggestions:

- A charming or whimsical lamp
- A vintage desk clock
- A hand-decorated journal
- A basket with ribbons woven through for your books and magazines
- Candles on the dresser or bathroom counter
- A quilt hanger for your grandmother's quilt
- Decorative wall shelves
- Glass-enclosed knickknack shelf
- Reading nook with standing lamp
- Basket of bath goodies

Search your house for treasures you can incorporate in new ways. Once you've got a vision for your rooms, then spend some time evaluating what's stopping you from being there already. What obstacles keep you from having the rooms of your dreams?

The Source of Clutter

If you stood at the door to your bedroom, what would you see? Would you see a treadmill doubling as a clothes hanger? Books on the floor? Bills strewn on the dresser? Laundry piled on the bed? Now, ask yourself: Why is it like that?

Here are some possible reasons:

- The closet is too full.
- The dressers are overstuffed.
- There aren't enough hangers.
- The linen cabinet is filled with games.
- You need a bigger jewelry case, or less jewelry.
- You need a bookcase, a bigger bookcase, or fewer books.

The answer to your clutter problem is somewhere in here. You probably know what it is, but you are avoiding it because of the domino effect. In other words, your clothes are draped over the tub because your closet is too full. Your closet is too full because your under-the-bed boxes are filled with things you don't wear anymore. One problem leads to another, and it's easier to avoid them all by doing nothing.

Perhaps the answer lies in solving one problem, while allowing another to sit until you can address it. You can't solve everything at once. But you can change something . . . even if it means loading books, magazines, and clothes into plastic tubs until you can figure out what to do with them.

To start, identify your biggest problems in your bedroom and bathroom and write them down. Your list might look like this:

- No place to hang a bathrobe.
- Not enough towel racks.
- Dresser drawers are full.
- Jewelry is all over the dresser.
- Exercise equipment you no longer use is taking up space.
- Books are all over the floor.

Once you've recorded the clutter sources, start to address them one by one. Success breeds success, and you'll be motivated to keep going. Following are some tips to help.

Bedroom Organizing Tips

Clutter can easily take over a bedroom. Especially when that room becomes the dumping ground in a mad attempt at cleaning before company arrives. To tackle this room, simply pick one project at a time. Little by little, you'll reclaim this space as your own. Consider starting with one of the following areas.

Minimize Visual Clutter

Avoid the temptation to install hooks or racks in your master bedroom, as these create visual clutter. Instead, move these items to the closet. The chapter on storage spaces covers options for hanging things like belts, hats, and scarves.

Bedside Table

If possible, invest in a bedside table with drawers. Drawers can store reading material, glasses, hand lotion, journal, pens, and television remote controls. Limit the number of items on top of your bedside table to a few books and magazines, plus your lamp and clock.

If you don't have the option of a bedside table with drawers, purchase a decorative box with a lid to store your nighttime accessories.

To get even more storage, consider putting a small dresser by your bed instead of a nightstand. Or if you are a reader, consider a specially designed reader's table, with multiple shelves for books and magazines.

Vanity

A vanity is a feminine touch that is also functional. Make sure you get one with plenty of drawer space. Your vanity can store makeup, lotions, perfume, and all those other products women use daily.

Store limited items on the top of your vanity. For those items on top, use a decorative container—ideally with a lid to reduce the visual clutter. Consider antique cream and sugar containers, vintage glassware, or other interesting items to hold Q-tips, cotton balls, and makeup brushes.

Under-the-Bed Storage

Fill every space under your bed with specially designed boxes. Spend a bit more to purchase the kind with wheels for ease of access. Make sure you measure the height of that space to avoid a second trip to the store. If you don't want to buy boxes, consider storing suitcases under the bed filled with items. Another option is space-saving bags. Use these to store items that are bulky, such as linens, comforters, or heavy winter outerwear. To hide this storage space, use a bed skirt.

Here are some ideas on what to store under your bed:

- Off-season clothing
- Seldom-worn dress clothes
- Shoes or boots
- Extra bedding
- Books, DVDs, or CDs
- Craft supplies
- Photo albums

Alternative Storage

If you need storage but don't have the budget or room for another piece of big furniture, consider these ideas for alternative storage:

- Hope chest or trunk. This can sit at the foot of the bed and doubles as a bench.
- Vintage or antique suitcases stacked on top of each other. These suitcases could hold blankets, winter clothes, or sweaters.
- Decorative covered boxes. Stack multiple boxes on top of each other. They can hold lightweight items like scarves, belts, and jewelry.
- Vintage picnic basket. Tuck the television remote, CDs, or DVDs in a picnic basket with lid.

Dresser

To make the most of the space you have, take the time to empty each drawer in your dresser. Consider the following tips:

- Store themed clothing elsewhere (exercise, pool/beach).
- Remove unwanted or off-season clothing.
- Match socks; discard singles.
- Discard stretched/torn/overly worn undergarments.
- Add drawer dividers to sort smaller items, like socks and underwear.

Jewelry

Don't forget your jewelry. For too many years I tossed my jewelry in a big box, which became a source of ongoing frustration when looking for something specific.

- Store jewelry sets (necklaces, earrings, and bracelets) in sandwich-sized, zip-top plastic bags. Then store flat in a decorative box.
- Use a hanging jewelry organizer with clear pockets.
- Use a jewelry roll and store in dresser.
- Use a pretty jewelry tree.
- Use a stacking organizer for small items.
- Store expensive jewelry in a safety deposit box.
- Take photographs of all valuable jewelry items. Store photographs with purchase date and price, or estimated value, in a photo album.

Books

If you are an avid reader, consider placing a bookshelf in your bedroom. Adding a hutch to the top of a dresser will save space. Or, go vertical and install wall-mounted shelves above a dresser. If you have an odd nook in your room, a built-in bookcase might be an answer.

Workspace

Since many bedrooms double as an office, invest in a desk or a secretary where you can hide your paperwork. When you need a peaceful retreat, the last thing you want to see is work. When done with work, clear the desktop or shut the secretary door.

Tabletop Valet

To corral small items like cufflinks, watches, wallets, and change, consider a valet. These tabletop accessories also come with chargers for electronics.

Ironing Center

If your ironing board is permanently set up in your bedroom, consider finding a home for it in your closet. Hang the board on a wall or tuck it behind clothing. Store the iron and other accessories in a portable tote. Place a basket for clothes needing to be ironed on the floor of the closet.

Morning Bedroom Maintenance Routine

- Say "good morning" to God.
- Thank him for a blessing (a new day is always good).
- Make your bed. This three-minute ritual is the jumpstart to an organized room. Fold blankets, carefully place decorative pillows, and smooth the comforter. You'll be energized to keep going.
- Hang up your robe.
- Put away pajamas.
- Put stray shoes in the closet.
- Put dirty clothes in the hamper.
- Hang up wearable clothes, or place in the ironing basket for a touch-up.
- Open curtains.
- Greet the day with a smile.

Bathroom Organizing Tips

The approach that worked on your bedroom can work on your bathroom. It doesn't all have to be organized in a day, so pick one project to address at a time. Here are some suggestions for bringing order and beauty to your bathroom.

Linen Closet

Store your towels, washcloths, and linens with the rounded folded edge facing out. This cleans up the look.

Medicine Cabinet

Keeping your medicine cabinet organized offers more than a decorative benefit. You will be happy to have bandages and salve on hand when someone takes a bad tumble. Here are a few suggestions:

- Remove all containers and clean shelves.
- Throw away empty bottles or tubes.
- Safely discard unused prescription medication. (Return to a pharmacy for safe disposal.)
- Consider storing medications away from the humidity of a bathroom.
- Discard products you won't use or don't like.
- Combine like products when safe to do so (like sunscreen).
- Replace items in similar groupings.
- Add tiered wire shelving for small items.
- Add labeled drawers for small items.
- Create kits: camping, manicure, beach, first aid.
- Make a list of emergency products to have on hand.

Under the Sink

Don't neglect to bring order to the space under the sink. By adding affordable stacking shelves, you can utilize every inch of vertical space. Consider baskets to contain items like curling irons and blow dryers.

Another option for storage is stacked drawers. These come in plastic, wire, or mesh and in various sizes.

Baskets

Place baskets on the edge of your tub with rolled towels, pretty soaps, or hair products.

Wall-Mounted Shelves

Add shelving over your bathtub or toilet for personal products or stacked towels.

Over-the-Toilet Cabinet

A freestanding cabinet over the toilet is a great place for extra towels or toilet paper.

Sharing a Room with Someone Messy

Not long after the wedding, I discovered a serious flaw in my husband: he dropped his clothes wherever he took them off. He left his shoes in front of the couch, socks by the bed, and workout clothes on the floor of the bathroom. No matter how many times I nagged, he still considered the house a hamper.

It wasn't that he was an inconsiderate husband. He was very thoughtful and caring in other areas. And he didn't expect me to pick up after him. He just didn't think about it. For a while, I simmered over what seemed like a personal attack and a lack of respect for how hard I worked. *Did he expect me to be his maid?*

There were three options: 1) continue to nag uselessly; 2) leave the clothes where they were and hope he eventually picked them up; or 3) consider it a loving act of service to clean up after him. Occasionally I get it right, and that was one of those times. I chose option three. Beginning that day, I picked up my husband's clothes.

I never told him what I was doing, and he never commented. Slowly things started to change. Honestly, I didn't even notice it until years later.

But at some point in those early years of marriage, my husband discovered the hamper. Now, twenty-six years later, he diligently picks up his clothes, and he sees that the children do, too.

This isn't the answer for everyone, nor can I promise the same outcome. But if your spouse if messy, you have the same options I did. If you want a clean bedroom, decide if it will be an act of service. Not only will you be serving your husband with love, but the Bible tells us we are actually serving the Lord as well. Ephesians 6:7–8 says, "Serve wholeheartedly, as if you were serving the Lord, not people, because you know that the Lord will reward each one for whatever good they do, whether they are slave or free."

Making sure the house is clean and organized is my calling in our family. Not that I do all the work—I don't. But I'm always trying to find new ways to help my family organize their belongings. This especially applies to my husband. I take my role as his helpmate seriously. Over the years, I've tried to make his life easier here and there . . . providing a place to hang his keys and a place for his sunglasses. And when those items are out of place, it's another act of service to place them where they belong without a word. It's a choice, and compared to the option of nagging, it's the better choice by far.

· ·

Chapter Eighteen

Functional Living Areas

· · · · · · · · · · ∞ · · · · · · · · · ·

When I worked at a retirement center years ago, before any public event we took a "Do you see what I see?" walk. We started at the street entrance and walked in the driveway. Our eyes scanned the parking lot, building, windows, and landscaping. We tried to look with fresh eyes at what a visitor would see. It was always interesting how noticeable the chipped paint, cobwebs, and dead bushes were from that viewpoint.

We had walked past them every day, never noticing. On that day, with intentional eyes, we saw what needed changing. Often it didn't take much to correct the problem. Armed with clipboards, paper, and pens we recorded every item needing attention and created a master to-do list.

Sensory adaptation is to blame for numbing us visually to things in our home as well. It's a God-given gift to adapt to our surroundings. Otherwise, we might be overwhelmed with aromas and sounds. It can also mean we live with more messes, chaos, and clutter than we should. Unless we perform our own "Do you see what I see?" walk, we'll miss small areas of our home that could be cleaned up with little effort.

In this chapter, we'll look at common living areas and consider solutions for bringing order to the places our families congregate most.

Define Your Purpose

Most rooms in the home have an obvious purpose—we cook in the kitchen and shower in the bathroom. To maximize organization and increase effectiveness of the general living areas, we may need to define their purposes. That way, we can consider whether things need to be moved from one room to another. For example, if your family plays games in the family room, but it's too much trouble to search through the bedroom toys for the board games, consider moving them closer.

You see, the goal of organization isn't to have a pristine home, it's to free you to live the life you want and to obey God's calling for you and your family. With that in mind, consider each general room in your home. Ask yourself two questions:

1) What does my family currently do in this room?
2) What do I wish my family could do in this room?

The answer to the first question will guide you in setting up activity zones for each room. It will help you decide what stays and what goes. But don't neglect the answer to the second question. If you long for your family to gather and read in the family room, then set that as a goal. Do you want to extend more hospitality, but it takes an army and a battle to clean up?

Let real life and your dreams guide your decision making. The answer is probably somewhere in between.

If you already feel overwhelmed, this might be difficult to do. If possible, find some time to be by yourself and think. Ask God to give you a vision for your home and living spaces. Organization should make it easier to accomplish your personal and family goals—not create one more thing to do. When I see organization as a path to greater family time and personal development, it's easier to cast a vision that will require work.

Armed with your reality and vision, consider the community areas in your home.

Entryway

Your front entrance sets the mood and first impression to your home. Will it be one of peace and rest? Or should there be flashing red lights and signs reading "Danger"? Does your entryway convey confident authority or disordered anarchy? Your family and guests will immediately receive the unspoken message.

Without a plan, entryways can become dumping grounds. Family members kick off shoes, drop bags, and toss keys. Most often, that happens because there isn't a safe place for those items. With a bit of rearranging, you can create a beautiful front entrance, one that offers a "welcome home" for your loved ones and their possessions. Following are some suggestions.

Keys

Provide key hooks or key racks within a few steps of the door. Make sure there are enough hooks for each member of your family. It's a good idea to store extra sets of all keys, but not at the front entrance. Invest in a key storage box, and put it in your laundry room or hang hooks inside a cabinet. Don't forget to label extra keys.

Back to the front entrance. If you've got room, consider getting an attractive wall-mounted holder with small hooks for keys. This might be a shelf, which you could also use to hold small items such as a wallet, money clip, or cell phone. Or it could be a letter holder with hooks at the bottom. This could hold incoming or outgoing mail, or small items to grab on the way out.

You might also consider getting a message board and adding hooks for keys. There are multiple possibilities for getting double duty out of a key holder, so don't limit your imagination.

Purses, Backpacks, Bags

The goal is to get purses, backpacks, and miscellaneous bags off the floor. To that end, position a coat tree or coat rack near the door. If you have little ones, include a child-sized coat rack or a double row of hooks with one row low enough for little arms. A hall tree (a bench with storage, a back, and hooks) is a great place to store items, plus provide a seat.

If you have an entry closet, make sure it's not jam-packed. Add shelving for purses and hooks for bags.

Loose Items

For books, mittens, iPods, or small bags, consider cubbyholes with baskets. Label a basket for each person in the family. This can serve many purposes, and it's an excellent way for everyone to keep track of little items. A table or small chest by the front door can be multifunctional. Place a basket on top for keys and use the drawers to store those little items that easily get lost.

Shoes

I know many people like to keep shoes by the front door. In case you do, some options include providing cubbyholes or baskets, instead of having them loose on the floor. However, may I respectfully recommend discontinuing that habit? Dirty shoes can mar your guests' first impressions—both visually and with a less-than-pleasant aroma. By providing adequate shoe storage in bedrooms, family members can remove shoes at the door and take shoes directly to their closets.

Community Rooms

How does your family live in your community rooms? If you haven't already, make a list of the different activities happening on a daily or weekly basis. It might look something like this:

- Study
- Work
- Play board games
- Watch television or movies
- Play video games

- Eat
- Entertain or extend hospitality
- Read
- Crafts

Is your home functional for these activities? What is working? What is not? And what types of clutter do you have? If things are strewn around the living areas, what are they? Blankets? Books? Magazines? Game controllers? Mail?

Think through every piece of clutter. In fact, you might even take a notebook and list every item that doesn't have a home. If things do have a home, but you or your family members aren't putting items away, perhaps you don't have an organization problem. Maybe it's more of a discipline problem. That just requires some simple habit changes. But even if discipline is the issue, organization can help.

While I love a good vision, I'm a realist at heart. There are seasons in our lives when we have to make things easy on ourselves. When my children were toddlers, I read somewhere to make changes in your home so you don't have to say no as often. That seemed brilliant to me, since I was sure everyone thought my oldest son's name was "No, Joshua!" I packed up breakables, removed things from lower shelves, and baby-proofed the house. It worked. My stress level decreased and everyone was happier.

If your family refuses to fold blankets or put books back on the shelf, accept it for now. Instead of being annoyed, find a convenient home for those items so you can easily pick up the room. You can work on establishing better habits later, and once your home is clutter-free, you might find everyone is more motivated to help.

Let's look at some tips for common clutter problems and practical ways for organizing your living areas.

Too Much Stuff

One reason our living areas get disorganized is too much stuff in too little space. This problem never gets better on its own. The older you get, the more items you accumulate with sentimental value. When my Grannie passed away, I inherited some of her treasured items. They added to the collection of other precious things.

Stuff piled on stuff equals more stuff. What to do with it all? Here are some ideas:

A glass-enclosed curio cabinet. Twenty years ago, my husband bought me a six-foot-high, two-foot-wide glass case. It sits right by my front door where I can see all my little treasures. And my treasures are safely tucked away and dust-free.

Give items to family now. If you've got children, nieces, or nephews, plan to share some of your treasures with them now. This can be an inexpensive Christmas or birthday gift. It blesses both of you.

Give items away. Find a ministry helping people be independent after a trauma, such as a battered women's shelter, refugee ministry, or recovery program. Your beloved items could bring hope and healing to someone else.

Sell on eBay or at a consignment center. If you need to make some money, consider selling your extra items. A good digital camera and packing material is all you need to sell online.

Books

Once every few years, sort through your books and discard what you don't need for reference or will never read again. I know books are like good friends. But they are also good to share with those who might not be able to afford a new book.

- Check with local schools, libraries, service organizations, and ministries to see who accepts books.
- Sell them used on Amazon.
- Give them away to friends.
- Donate like-new books to your church to use as door prizes.
- Sell them as a fundraiser for your favorite ministry. My mother's church holds a book sale every year to raise funds for their women's retreat. I always have bags to give her.

For those books you want to keep, consider adding bookshelves. Build shelves into an unused nook. Dedicate a wall of a study for built-ins or large bookshelves. Tuck a two-shelf case under a window. Anywhere you have wall space, you can build a bookcase.

Remote Controls

Do your remote controls have legs like mine do? If so, you'll appreciate having a home for them. Here are some suggested tips:

- Store remotes in a decorative box on the coffee table.
- Buy or make a fabric remote holder that fits over the arm of a couch or chair.
- Install a wall-mounted basket by the television.
- Put a box or basket by the television.

Blankets

- A chest of drawers can serve as an end table and storage for items like blankets.
- Position a quilt hanger by the couch.
- A vintage-looking sea chest can double as a coffee table and blanket holder.

Magazines

Place only current magazines on top of tables. Store older issues in a basket, tucked at the end of the couch or under a table. Buy some decorative magazine holders for those issues you want to keep long-term, and place them in a bookcase.

For magazines you really don't want to keep, establish an exit plan. I've got some ideas in Chapter Thirteen on overcoming paper clutter.

Craft Supplies and Games

These items can take up lots of space. Store them in stacking boxes to make the most of your space. Consider storing games behind the closed doors of an armoire or entertainment center to minimize visual clutter. If the game box is damaged, transfer game boards and pieces to specially designed plastic game keepers sold at specialty organizing stores (www. organizeit.com).

For crafts, consider a rolling organizer with multiple drawers that can be tucked in a closet while not in use. A cubby system with boxes covered in wallpaper to match your design could fit nicely in a niche. Make labels for each drawer or box.

Toys

Unless you have a designated playroom, keep most toys in bedrooms. For a quick pickup, keep a large basket with a lid in the living room. Rolling bins make cleanup fun when a child can roll it back to her room.

Multimedia

Plastic boxes multiply like rabbits in a home with growing children. Whether it's a CD, DVD, or video game box, it needs to be stored in a crush-proof place. Consider adding pull-out drawers to deep shelving so that items in the back can be easily seen. A specially designed media tower protects boxes and keeps the titles visible.

Little Treasures

After my father passed away, my mother created shadow boxes for my sister and me. She carefully arranged little items my father collected over the years in these boxes. For example, she included his army pins, a pipe, and his school ID. If you've got little treasures that can get lost or broken, consider creating your own themed shadow box.

Framed Photos

Consider hanging a collage of photos on the wall instead of cluttering the surface of an end table or sofa table with frames. Choose a common frame color and complementary matting to make a design statement.

Extra Storage Options

Instead of pushing your couch against the wall, consider putting a table or chest of drawers there instead. Then, pull the couch out so there's enough room to walk behind. This gives extra storage, plus adds room for lovely touches of beauty.

Make furniture do double-duty. Invest in accent tables with shelves and drawers. If that's not an option, store items in large baskets tucked under tables. A chest can serve as a coffee table or a bench with cushions.

Remember to go up. Buy furniture that gives you extra vertical storage space. When possible, consider a built-in option. Built-ins save space, can go to the ceiling for complete use of space, and can match your interior design in style and color.

Creating a comfortable, welcoming home is a priority goal for me. It's not about interior design or having a floor you can eat off of; it's more about the heart of the hostess and stress-free places to gather. If your heart longs for a home where family and friends breathe a sigh of relief upon entering, then consider starting your organizing with your common areas. It will make a big impact in the shortest amount of time.

Chapter Nineteen

. . . .

Closets and Storage Spaces

. . . .

The closets are often the last area of a home to be addressed. They are like the pain in your shoulder you ignore, until you can't type or play tennis. Then, with a heavy sigh of resignation, you call the doctor. Instead of waiting until closets are serious problems, take the proactive step of tackling them.

Storage spaces are the foundation of home organization. Items stay permanently on counters, floors, and dressers because they have no other place to go. Years ago, a friend told me she couldn't unload her dish drainer because there wasn't space in her cupboards for the plates. This plagues us all sometimes. That's why diving into the dark spaces of our homes is critical.

If you think your problem is not enough closet space, you could be right. However, the reality is, unless you have a custom-designed home (or are already well organized), no one thinks she has enough storage. Why? Stuff expands to fill empty space. So almost all of our closets, cabinets, and garages get filled to capacity. We delay making decisions about things when we don't have the space to store them. So, we stack boxes on the floor of a closet, pile bags on top of each other, or throw things in bins. It's easier.

That works until it doesn't. When our clothes are smashed and wrinkled, when we can't find winter gloves, and when we spend money on gifts we forgot we'd already bought—then we realize it's time to do something about those black holes. Then we are forced to make decisions. Hopefully the chapter on clutter offered some helpful tips on processing your possessions. It can be painful to release things you've loved, but you will be lighter in spirit afterward.

Whether you have a tiny coat closet or a huge walk-in closet, you can manage your storage space wisely. The trick is to make the most of every inch you have available. Top to bottom, side to side, there is unused, or underused, space in every closet and garage. Here are some tips to help make the most of what you have.

General Tips

As you prepare to organize a closet, start by assessing unused or unwisely used space. Look up toward the ceiling. Look down on the floor. Look at every inch of wall space. Consider if there is room for an installed shelf, stacking removable shelves, a chest of drawers, or cubbies. Vertical space is usually underused and an easy fix.

Closets don't always have to be completely reorganized. Identify those areas that *aren't* working for you now. Are clothes jam-packed? Shoes in piles? Scarves slipping off shelves? You may not have to rearrange your entire closet, just a few areas. Pick one section at a time to organize, and you won't feel quite so overwhelmed.

The goal is for contents to be:

1. Viewed.
2. Easily accessed.
3. Labeled when not in view.

Can you find what you need in your closet? Maybe things are organized, but you just need labels on containers. Spend some time thinking about what really gets on your nerves and start there.

The problem most of us have is too much stored in too little space. It's likely you'll need to permanently remove some items from your closets in order to provide functional storage. The truth is many of us have a close relationship with our clothes that makes it hard to think logically. Here are some tips to help you process those difficult clothing decisions.

Bedroom Closets

A bedroom closet is the place of dreams. Dreams that we can still fit into *that* dress, that we will wear *those* heels, or that someday our favorite pink shirt will actually look good on us. Clothing is associated with special events and seasons of our lives, and it is very difficult to give up. Having to admit that I'm older and can't wear certain styles is painful. Organizing my bedroom closet means I might have to let those dreams go. However, I've found a way to make it easier.

When I find it hard to part with a skirt I once loved, there's an image I bring to my mind. It motivates me to make the right decision. The image is of a single mother who is trying to get a job. She knows she needs to provide for her daughter, but she doesn't have anything nice to wear, nor the money to run to the mall and pick up a cute outfit. She needs something. Then I look at the lovely skirt I no longer wear. That skirt can either hang in my closet gathering dust, or it can help a sister I haven't met. I don't know who she is, but I have things that can help her.

The early followers of Jesus inspire me in this quest to share my belongings with others. Acts 2:44–56 describes this important part of living out their faith. "All the believers were together and had everything in common. They sold property and possessions to give to anyone who had need." They trusted God to provide their needs, and he did, often through the giving of others.

Keeping an open hand with my resources helps me keep perspective when I want to hang on to something longer than I should. As you look at your own closet, hopefully this imagery will help loosen the hold clothes have.

Organizing your closet can be done in three easy steps:

1. Relocate items that should or could be stored elsewhere.
2. Remove clothing you don't want.
3. Reorganize what is left.

Within each step, there are multiple decisions; hopefully the rest of this section will provide a helpful guide and tips.

Relocate What Can Be Stored Elsewhere

Sometimes our closets are catchalls for miscellaneous items. As you evaluate the odds and ends in your storage spaces, consider if it would make more sense to store them elsewhere. When possible, put items close to where they are used.

Move items to another room. Try to keep like items together and in a logical space. If you've stored files or kitchen appliances in your bedroom closet, remove those. Hopefully you have more room for stray objects, as you bring order to your home.

Remove items you seldom wear. This might be formal wear or ski clothes. These items can be stored in an attic or garage. If you have room, consider storing seldom-used hanging items on a rolling garment rack. Buy one with a clear or fabric zipped covering. For under a hundred dollars, you can get a large portable wardrobe with rods for hanging and places for shoes and other folded clothing.

Remove off-season clothing. Store these items under the bed or in another dresser. Or consider a portable garment rack tucked in a garage or workroom.

If there is absolutely no more room in your house, consider temporary storage options. Renting a mini-storage space could be a short-term option. A small size is about 5' by 5' and price ranges are based on your city. An average monthly cost for that size is around forty dollars. Watch for specials, pay up front for a discount, or share it with a friend.

Remove What You Don't Wear

Admit it. Most of us hold on to things longer than we should. There are probably complicated emotional reasons why we do what we do. Sentimentality is a big one. Dreams, mentioned earlier, is another. To get to a place of efficiency in our closets, we must remove things that shouldn't be there or anywhere else in our homes.

If you don't use certain things because they need repair, that's different. Sort through those items and either fix them yourself (go to a fabric store for supplies), or research alteration and repair options. Besides what can be repaired, remove clothing that falls into any of the following categories.

Damaged or stained beyond repair. Repurpose these clothes when possible. Use scraps for dusting or arts and crafts. Give usable pieces to quilters you know. Make clothing into other items like purses or tote bags. Set some aside to use as cleanup rags for messy or dirty jobs such as yard work, cleaning, or projects.

Not my style. No matter how much you love them, remove clothes you don't wear due to style. Fifteen years after working outside the house, my dress clothes still hung in my closet. Even if I could have fit into them, they weren't my personal style anymore. Or, the pieces were too "young" for me. A fashion expert once said women over thirty shouldn't wear two things: dresses with bows in the back and jumpers. I could have cried! Since I tend to ignore "expert" advice, I could have laughed and kept wearing my comfortable dresses. But they really weren't flattering. It was hard, but I passed those items along for others to enjoy.

Not worn. Shari Braendel, author of *Good Girls Don't Have to Dress Bad*, wrote in an article for the *P31 Woman* magazine, "Without emotion, take everything out of your closet you have not worn in the last 18 months. The reason for the 18-month rule is that this gives you two seasons of the previous one you just went through. For example, if summer has just ended and you have things hanging in your closet that you didn't wear this year

OR the summer before, chances are you are not going to wear it next year."[1]
I like Shari's advice better than the typical one-year rule.

Undecided. Some items of clothing present a challenge. We don't love
them, nor hate them. Professional organizer and *Mission: Organization*
guest Monica Ricci offers this piece of advice:

> Go through the 'undecided' pile piece by piece, and ask yourself
> what value each piece currently gives you. Warning: Do not get
> sucked in by the clothing trying to convince you of its value and
> reminding you how good you used to look wearing it. Clothing
> is sly and it will say anything to get you to keep it around. It
> will remind you of how expensive it was, or that it was a gift
> from your mother-in-law, but do not fall for these sneaky tricks!
> You must be strong and objective. Clothes that aren't serving
> you need to be culled to make room for those pieces that are
> valuable.[2]

Wrong size. We have the opportunity to look stylish at any age or
weight. If there are clothes that don't fit well, or not at all, let them go. I
highly recommend Shari Braendel's book, *Good Girls Don't Have to Dress
Bad*. It's a full-color, step-by-step guide for every height and shape.

Of course, keeping some things makes sense if you are on a weight
loss plan. Just be honest with yourself.

Reorganize

Now that your closet is simplified, it will be much easier to organize
what's left.

Shoes. Proper shoe care will extend their life. Keep them separated
by pair and protected from scuff marks by dirty soles. Options include:

- Over-the-door hangers.
- Cubbies on the ground or on shelves.
- Shoe racks on the ground. These can be stacked to make the
  most of your space.

- Shoe boxes—either clear or labeled.
- Under-the-bed storage for boots and seldom-worn shoes.
- Revolving shoe tree (visit www.organize.com).

Hanging items. Devise a simple organization plan for sorting your clothes. Most organizers recommend keeping like items together, such as slacks, skirts, and blouses. Then sort by color. It will make it easier to see how many white, long-sleeved shirts you have before you buy another.

Add additional hanging space by using a double hanging rod. Professional organizer Eileen Koff writes, "If your clothes are crammed together like a can of sardines, the best approach is to get more hanging space. Hanging rods that hook over existing rails are a smart, inexpensive, and an instant way to create extra room for short hanging clothes."[3]

Sweaters. Fold sweaters and stack on shelves. Install dividers to create vertical control over spillage. Specially designed, soft-sided sweater boxes have clear fronts to see contents and ease stacking. Organize by color, type (cardigan or pullover), or weight (spring or winter).

Belts, scarves, and ties. Use a hanging device with multiple arms, or mount one on the back of your closet door. Look for a product with a nonslip surface on the arms. Sort items by color.

Linen Closet

Are you afraid to open your linen closet doors for fear of what will slip and slide out? You aren't alone. This space houses many hard-to-fold items, and most of us struggle with bringing order to the variety of sizes, shapes, and textures stored here. Perhaps some of these tips will help.

- Store sheets and pillowcase sets in shallow plastic boxes. Label the front with bed size.
- Store sheet sets in one pillowcase.
- Hang ironed tablecloths from padded hangers or skirt or trouser hangers. Put matching napkins in a gallon zip-top plastic bag and pin to the top of the hanger.

- Antique linens require extra care. Keep them professionally cleaned and stored in archival paper.
- Use stacking baskets for towels and washcloths.
- Consider space saver bags for seasonal items like beach towels or winter blankets.
- Store larger items in zippered bags. Consider square bags to make the most of space.
- Guard against bugs by cleaning items before storing.

Hall Closet

Perhaps a good place to start with a hall or entry closet is to define your purpose. Would you like to use this space as a place for guests' coats? Do you use it every day for your own items? Sometimes this little gem is overlooked, and it becomes a haphazard storage place for that grab-and-dash cleaning some of us do right before company arrives.

With a bit of planning, your hall closet has great potential for being a one-stop organizing center for items that get brought in and taken out on a regular basis. For example, you could add additional shelves and store camera equipment. Hooks on the inside of the door could be used for purses and bags. Cubbies or stacked baskets on the floor could hold books, backpacks, shoes, and gloves. Install hooks on the inside of the door for keys.

By putting some effort into redesigning your hall closet, you'll create a home for lots of common clutter problems.

. . . .

Chapter Twenty

Organizing Children's Rooms and Treasures

. . . . ∽ . . . .

Frustrated with the mess, I once asked my daughter to "organize her room." Quiet reigned as she diligently worked. An hour later, curious about her progress, I slipped down the hall, peeked in, and saw her head bent in concentration. I also saw the closet empty, clothing and hangers spread over the floor, her bed draped with books and toys, and the dresser piled high with more stuff. Her heart was in the right place, but the more she "organized," the more overwhelming the project became.

It was another reminder that organization isn't a skill that is taught once, then caught forever. It's an ongoing process to teach children how to categorize items and make discriminating decisions about what should go where.

Asking my daughter to organize her room by herself was too big a request. I stepped into the mess and, in a short while, we had set the room to rights. I shouldn't have assigned her the task in annoyance, nor asked her to work alone. In doing so, I almost missed an opportunity to model the helpful life skills of sorting, making decisions, and brainstorming solutions.

In the past, I've set up organizational systems my children had trouble maintaining. Now, as I consider ideas for each child's space, I ask myself this question: Can my child maintain this? If your mile-a-minute son won't take the time to carefully place pairs of shoes in a shoe-keeper, consider a basket or bin he can throw them in as he races to the next event.

There are no right or wrong organizing practices. What works for one child won't work for another. Become a student of your child, and understand how she thinks. What would make the most sense to her? How does she process information? Armed with that information, you'll be better equipped to bring order to your child's room.

Identify Problems Together

Before jumping in to "help" your child organize his room, have a brainstorming session. Together, discuss problems with the room as it is. Ask your child if he has any trouble finding things or knowing where to put things. Make a list of the problem areas as he sees it. Many children feel protective about their rooms, since that space is one of the few things they call their own. Enlisting their help in problem solving will get you an ally when change happens.

Create Activity Zones

One idea for organizing a child's room is to create activity zones. These zones serve as logical "homes" for different items. As you identify functions for different areas of the room, you'll find it easier to make storage decisions.

If your child loves to draw, then an art center is the perfect place for a washable rug, well-worn worktable, easel, chair, and rolling multi-drawer cart to store paper, crayons, paints, and other supplies.

For a child who loves to read, a comfy chair, standing lamp, and bookcase filled with books is the perfect reading zone.

Activity zones in your child's room might include:

- Rest
- Play
- Arts and crafts projects
- Reading
- Study
- Dressing
- Primping (makeup table)
- Make-believe/dress-up
- Music

Storage Options

Consider every space in your child's room as potential storage. Vertical space is often overlooked. Here are some suggestions:

- **Wire or wicker drawers** to tuck in narrow spaces. Store clothes, toys, or school supplies in these drawers. If your child has uniforms for sports or performing arts, consider keeping those clothes stored separately.
- **Rolling plastic drawer cart**. It can be rolled out for easy cleanup, then tucked in the closet under hanging clothes.
- **Furniture with extra storage**, such as:
  - A nightstand with drawers.
  - A storage bed, with multiple drawers below the mattress.
  - A footstool with a lid.
  - A headboard with shelves.
- **Cedar chest** at the foot of the bed (can double as a bench). These are great places to store extra blankets, pillows, or winter outerwear.
- **Built-in bookcases**. Consider wall-to-wall bookcases. This is a safer option for small children and potentially a more affordable one for do-it-yourselfers. We did this once, and it was a great option. We added four shelves, painted them

the same color as the walls, and utilized every inch of that wall for storage space.

- **Shelving around the top of the walls.** Our growing athletes accumulated trophies and other sports memorabilia. Instead of cluttering dresser tops, we installed decorative shelving around the perimeter of the room, approximately fifteen inches below the ceiling. Now their collectible items are safely stored and proudly displayed.
- **Coat trees** for backpacks, umbrellas, and jackets.

Labels

Labeling drawers, baskets, and boxes helps kids learn to categorize and provides a guide for cleaning up. If your child isn't reading yet, consider photos or drawings of what goes where. Be creative with labels. You can go vintage with a string tag, professional with a label machine, or creative with stickers or hand-drawn letters. Cute labels can be part of your decorating plan.

Bulletin Board

A large bulletin board is a multipurpose organizing tool. Not only can it hold photos and drawings, but it can store tickets, coupons, and reminder notes. With the right pushpins, it can hold necklaces, bracelets, or rings.

Wall Calendar

Start your child on a lifelong habit of keeping track of upcoming events and responsibilities on a calendar. On Sunday, review the week ahead, adding important events such as tests, evening programs, or parties. Your child can check this daily and prepare accordingly.

Storage for Tiny Things

It seems kids are always collecting little things. And tiny things get lost easily. For those little treasures, consider these ideas:

- Clear kitchen canisters
- Hardware organizers (the kind that holds nails and screws)
- Clear plastic jars
- Over-the-door jewelry holder
- Spice rack
- Jewelry box

Organizing Toys

Not only do we want to teach organization, but we also want to teach an appreciation for everything God gives us. We can use toys as an example of how to care for God's gifts. Instead of throwing toys in a chest, showing children how to store and maintain toys will plant seeds of responsibility for other possessions.

One tip for keeping toys manageable is to rotate the toys available to your child. Perhaps you might put out one-third of the toys, while storing the rest. Then, every so often, rotate them. Your child will be more interested in playing with "new" toys.

Open Storage Containers

Open containers such as baskets, boxes, and bins are great for storing toys that are bulky or oddly shaped. Consider investing in storage containers that complement your decorating scheme, such as vintage fruit boxes or fabric-lined baskets.

Plastic Game Savers

If your board game boxes are toast, consider a plastic "game saver." This is a plastic box specifically designed to hold a board, playing pieces, and cards. You'll find this product in a specialty organizing store.

Zip-Top Plastic Bags

Toys that have multiple parts can often be stored in zip-top bags. These are ideal for puzzles, LEGO creations, and Barbie outfits.

Hanging Chain with Clips

For hats, scarves, or small stuffed animals, consider a hanging chain with clips. This device can be fastened to a wall or hung in the closet.

Toy Hammock

Hang your child's stuffed animals in a toy hammock suspended from the ceiling or walls.

Puzzles

After your child has put together a puzzle, have her color the back of every piece with the same color. This way, if a piece strays, she knows where it belongs. Other ideas include assigning a number to each puzzle, or a symbol (like a heart). If you put your puzzle in a zip-top bag, tuck a piece of paper with that color into the bag, or write the number or symbol in a permanent marker on the bag.

Dressers

Put dividers in drawers to help keep socks, underwear, and bras in order. Dividers are expandable and come in shapes, such as diamonds or squares. Use them in any drawer that needs order.

Give Before Getting

The Bible teaches that it's better to give than receive (Acts 20:35). One way to help your child apply this lesson is to build times of giving into your year—ideally before a time of receiving gifts. If you exchange gifts at occasions like birthdays and Christmas, consider establishing a practice of giving beforehand. With your child, identify unneeded toys, books, clothing, jewelry, and other items (in excellent shape) to give away. Have your child help clean the items, if necessary, and identify the recipient. Consider a charity, neighbor, younger child, or family in need. Deliver the items together.

Not only is it a good practice to regularly pare down possessions, but it's a good character-building exercise.

Memory Boxes

As your child grows, you'll want to save mementos, figurines, or special outfits. Purchase storage boxes specifically for these items. These boxes need to be big enough to last through the years. As you remove items from your child's room to place in the memory box, be sure to wrap them securely. Photographs should be placed in acid-free envelopes. Store these boxes in a dry, cool place. If you have more than one child, clearly mark the box and each item to remove confusion in years to come.

Each of my children has two boxes in their closets. One is a memory box and the other is for school papers. The next tip explains what goes in that box.

Children's School Papers

With our first child, we saved everything! Every handprint made into a turkey and coloring page is priceless. Unless you have lots of storage, this may get difficult as the years go on and as you have more children. To keep your kids and you organized, here are some tips that work for us.

Purchase a colored pocket folder for each child. Every year, we get welcome letters from the teacher, classroom rules, student lists, and a school handbook. To keep that information handy, yet organized, I purchase an inexpensive colored pocket folder for each child. These folders lie flat in a kitchen drawer, ready for easy access.

Create another file for school items you want to save each school year. In our permanent file drawers, each child also has his or her own hanging file. Because it's not feasible to save everything, I have some criteria for what gets saved:

- Something that shows my child's development at that age
- Papers with teacher notes of praise
- A few papers (not many) that show an area of struggle
- Something that shows my child's uniqueness, such as drawings, stories, or poems

File the year's papers away. At the end of the school year, purchase 9" by 12" see-through expandable plastic envelopes from the office supply store. Most school papers fit inside this envelope. Put your child's school picture in the front, along with a piece of paper stating the school year. These can be easily stored in an under-the-bed box or a designated school box.

Share school papers with interested family members. To help out-of-state grandparents or other family members keep in touch with your child's development, consider sending some of the school papers and drawings to them. To ease the process, keep 9" by 12" addressed envelopes at the ready, and mail them once a month. Another tip is to write a letter on the back of the drawings, making them into homemade cards.

Step-by-Step Plan

If your child's room seems overwhelming to you, perhaps a step-by-step approach would help.

Step One: Gather Organizing Supplies

- Large, dark garbage bags. (Don't use see-through bags, or your child may change his mind about throwing or giving away beloved toys once he sees them in the "garbage.")
- Boxes or plastic bins for:
  o Recycling.
  o Items to give away.
  o Toys to temporarily store.
  o Seasonal clothing.
  o Items to give back to a friend.
  o Items to take to another room or repair.
- Basic organizing accessories like:
  o Over-the-door shoe keeper.
  o Under-the-bed box.
  o Closet organizers for belts, purses, hats, etc.

Place these bags and boxes (except for basic accessories) in the hallway or just outside the room. As you identify an item that doesn't belong in the room, place it in one of the bags or boxes. Removing these items from the room will help you feel a sense of accomplishment and minimize potential distress during the next step of reviewing and removing items.

Step Two: Clothes

- Remove outgrown items.
- Remove items needing alterations.
- Remove off-season clothing.
- Throw away clothing that is too damaged or stained to share.

Step Three: Toys

- Sort toys and games and put items in categories (blocks, cars, doll clothes, etc.).
- Put stray game pieces in the correct box.
- Throw away broken or incomplete toys or games.
- Identify toys to give away.
- Identify toys to store for the future.

Step Four: Paper

- Sort through stray papers.
- Recycle unneeded paper.
- Place in piles according to age or grade.
- Label with child's name and age or year.
- Store in appropriate files.

Step Five: Miscellaneous Items

- Sort any miscellaneous items by category: makeup, jewelry, hair products, cologne, desk supplies.
- Toss or give away unneeded items.
- Reassign homes.

Step Six: Assess Storage Needs

Once you've trimmed down your child's room, then consider storage options like those mentioned in this chapter.

Even with the most organized room, there's no guarantee your child will turn into a neatnik. But you'll know you've helped equip your children with basic organizing skills to take with them as they grow.

Section Five

You Can Do It!

Chapter Twenty-One

Keeping It Real

To end this book, I'm going to change the pace and flavor. I want to leave you with encouragement from the Word of God for the challenges you will face to bring order and peace into your life and home. You see, if I added up all my words, no matter how well-written they may be, they are still incomparable to the impact and power of one Word from God.

To stay on course and live a life of priorities, order, and peace, we will need strength beyond ourselves. Many don't believe that and are certain of their own power. I know—I lived that way for many years. Believing in your own strength keeps you walking on a path parallel to a life of victory.

Getting organized is hard work. Bringing order to your home is a challenge. Learning to say no takes guts. Insecurity plagues the most confident woman at times. We need help.

No matter how many times you've tried to get organized before, know that today is a brand-new day. Leave behind your past failures and weaknesses. You are the only one who places limits on your ability or disqualifies you because of your past.

"Only with God can you start over more than once with an unblemished, untarnished, 100 percent, still-intact potential . . . the same

Potential He has always intended you to fulfill," said Liberty Savard in her book *Shattering Your Strongholds*.[1]

Those powerful words echo God's vision for you. And mine as well. Here is some encouragement for finishing well.

Learn to Finish Well

I love to start projects. Earlier in the book, I wrote about how I loved to start clubs when I was young. What I don't remember is those clubs lasting more than a week. That was partly because I was soon on to the next project. And probably because my friends and little sister got tired of me always being the boss. I had lots to learn about leadership, but back then, I was happy to start something new and be in charge.

Great intentions are easy, but establishing consistent follow-through has taken years of work. I've learned a lot from Jesus about finishing well. There's a passage in John 4 about Jesus speaking with a woman at the town well. Jesus spoke with the woman while his disciples entered the village. The conversation has deep importance, but something happened after it that I want you to read.

Jesus' disciples joined him just as the discussion ended and urged Jesus to eat. Jesus replied by telling them he had food they didn't know about. "'My food,' said Jesus, 'is to do the will of him who sent me and to finish his work'" (John 4:34).

We know from reading the Gospels that Jesus finished God's work in spite of hardship, persecution, betrayal, lies, physical torture, and an agonizing death. We have eternal life because Jesus finished well.

We have the opportunity to finish well when God calls us to obey. Don't minimize the task God has called you to. You may think organizing your husband's half of the closet is a waste of time. God has a pattern of using what seems insignificant to accomplish the magnificent. Your part is faithfulness and he'll do the rest.

God calls us to finish well, and Jesus modeled it. Sometimes finishing well means getting our hands dirty in life and doing things we don't want to do. But finishing well always means pleasing the Lord with commitment and obedience.

For Every Yes There Is a No

It always surprises me that there is a limit to my abilities. Seems I'm not Superwoman. In moments of optimism, I dream of becoming a slimmed down, spiritually mature, and more well-read version of myself. Living out those goals is infinitely more challenging.

That's because every time I set a goal for myself, a more appealing alternative presents itself. Have you noticed this phenomenon? Just as you decide to diet, someone brings you a plate of brownies they baked "just for you." As soon as you decide to get up early and pray, the cold weather makes it much more appealing to stay in bed. And that decision to stop gossiping gets challenged when some interesting news about your boss finds its way to your inbox.

Every good intention will be met with a challenge at some point. Without a plan, most of us will abandon those intentions, telling ourselves we knew we couldn't do it. Why did we even try?

The reason this happens is we overlook the fact that every "yes" we say to one thing requires a "no" to something else. Without that understanding, we operate outside of how life works and underestimate the cost of achieving our goals.

Here's an example of what I mean. When you say yes to reading your Bible every day, you have to say no to the morning news or your favorite novel. If you say yes to teaching a small group of women, you'll say no to your favorite Tuesday night TV show, plus give up free time to prepare.

As you say yes to bringing order to your schedule and home, identify where will you need to say no. This effort will take time away from something else. It will take mental focus. It will take sacrifice.

There will always be a sacrifice when we desire to move forward in an area of our lives. Goals are exciting. Possibility of change is alluring. Sacrifice is hard, but it's worth it in the big picture of our lives. In fact, it's the road Jesus called his followers to walk daily. In Luke 9:23, Jesus said: "Whoever wants to be my disciple must deny themselves and take up their cross daily and follow me."

The decision you are making to reclaim your former organized self is outstanding. And I applaud your positive thoughts and optimism. Just remember when you reach a plateau, or hit a dead end, perhaps it's time to evaluate if you've said "no" enough.

Face "Hard" Well

You know what "hard" feels like. I'm not talking about the feel of stone by a river or concrete under your feet. I'm talking emotionally hard . . . spiritually hard. The kind of hard that makes you want to give up, go back to bed, or slip into some sort of temporary abandonment of reality. If you feel overwhelmed and overwrought, you aren't alone.

Not only do we all feel that way at times, but God recorded stories of faithful men and women throughout the ages who felt that way, too. The book of Job in the Old Testament tells the story of someone who knew hard. It's surely one of the most difficult to read because God removed his hand of protection and allowed all the pain that Job experienced. In fact, God even pointed Job out to Satan as blameless, which Satan twisted into a challenge to bring Job down.

Confident in Job, God allowed the testing. So one by one, Satan destroyed that which was dear to Job: his family, health, and possessions. Then, just when you think it couldn't get any worse, Job's wife and friends step in to "help" with the most unhelpful advice. Job is beset on all sides, and at times he is ready to give up, even asking God to "crush" him and relieve him of misery.

Job was a good and honest man. A man of high integrity, he didn't deserve the hard times he experienced. Yet, in spite of unrelenting agony, Job battled to hold on to truth—truth about his feelings and truth about God. In spite of confusion and questions, Job refused to curse God. Though Job didn't understand why he was suffering, he chose to walk in honesty and integrity, believing God would bring something good out if it.

Job faced "hard" head on. He wobbled a bit, but then he planted his feet and steadfastly held on to faith that his God who had never abandoned him before would not do so now. No matter what he lost, and who abandoned him, Job knew God would always be with him. His emotions may have pulled a bit on this, but Job kept steering back to center. Job faced "hard" well.

To declare his faith, Job spoke words that echo through generations, off the lips of saints of old and suffering saints today: "I know that my redeemer lives, and that in the end he will stand on the earth" (Job 19:25).

Job's story has a happy ending. After he passed the testing, the Bible says, "The Lord blessed the latter part of Job's life more than the former part" (Job 42:12a). Although Job had to go through the hard times, and there were no easy answers, the Lord never abandoned him.

The good news is Job's story can be ours. Not that we would wish such catastrophe on ourselves, but we all face our own "hard." And Job's Redeemer is our Redeemer. If you are facing something hard today, Job's story can bring you comfort and hope, for our Redeemer lives!

Deal with Hurdles

I watched the 100-meter Olympic hurdle race in stunned amazement. How could this happen? The favorite to win the race, the world's top-ranked woman hurdler, fell heavily upon the ground after tripping over the first hurdle. Her pain was evident, her frustration clear as she refused to lift her head, clenched her fists, and limped off the track.

My heart ached for this woman who had devoted her life to the sport. She was focused, competent, and highly trained and had sacrificed much to get to the pinnacle of amateur track and field. Yet one mistake, one misjudgment, one miscalculation ended her chance of winning.

The similarities between a race and life are striking. In fact, the writer of Hebrews speaks of the Christian life in terms of a race in chapter 12, verse 1: "Therefore, since we are surrounded by such a great cloud of witnesses, let us throw off everything that hinders and the sin that so easily entangles. And let us run with perseverance the race marked out for us."

I believe that, for the Christian, life is like a hurdle race. Whether you face one hurdle or ten, to be effective in life, you need to know how to get over the hurdles. Unlike a normal hurdle race, where the barricade-like structures are strategically placed and obvious, hurdles in life pop up in the most surprising places and catch us off guard. Unfortunately, even the most spiritually mature woman can be surprised by her reaction to life's challenges.

The good news is that the hurdles we face are no surprise to God. He's not wringing his hands wondering how we're going to get over the current challenge or finish our race. In fact, he's already got the solution to every challenge we'll face, and he even sent us a model for soaring over them.

Hebrews 12:1b–3 offers hope for those struggling with the hurdles in life. It involves keeping our eyes on Jesus and learning from him. The verses say, "And let us run with perseverance the race marked out for us, fixing our eyes on Jesus, the pioneer and perfecter of faith. For the joy set before him he endured the cross, scorning its shame, and sat down at the right hand of the throne of God. Consider him who endured such opposition from sinners, so that you will not grow weary and lose heart."

To finish our race well, we need to cast off every weight and sin that hinders us from completing God's call on our lives. This makes it sound like an easy task: simply shake off our leg irons of sin and other burdens. However, John Derby got it right when he said, "When we keep our eyes on Jesus, nothing is easier; when we are not looking at Him, nothing more impossible."

◇ ◇ ◇

As I said at the beginning of this book, I'm on a journey to discover God's best for my life. Being productive with my time and a good steward of my resources are keys. Managing the details of life well allows me to live the rest of my life with less stress and more joy.

May the Lord be your strength, may he bless you with clear thoughts and his wisdom, and may you find joy in your journey to discover God's best for you.

About Proverbs 31 Ministries

If you were inspired by *I Used to Be So Organized* and yearn to deepen your own personal relationship with Jesus Christ, I encourage you to connect with Proverbs 31 Ministries. Proverbs 31 Ministries exists to be a trusted friend who will take you by the hand and walk by your side, leading you one step closer to the heart of God through:

- Encouragement for Today, online daily devotions
- The *P31 Woman* monthly magazine
- A daily radio program
- Books and resources
- Dynamic speakers with life-changing messages
- Online communities
- Gather and grow groups

To learn more about Proverbs 31 Ministries or to inquire about having Glynnis Whitwer speak at your event, call 877-731-4663 or visit www. Proverbs31.org.

Notes

Chapter Two

1. David Allen, *Getting Things Done: The Art of Stress-Free Productivity* (New York: Penguin Group, 2001), 22.

2. Edward M. Hallowell, "Overloaded Circuits: Why Smart People Underperform," *Harvard Business Review*, January 2005, 55–56.

3. Ibid.

Chapter Three

1. Rick Warren, *The Purpose Driven Life* (Grand Rapids, MI: Zondervan, 2002), 31.

Chapter Four

1. Carol Brazo, *No Ordinary Home* (Sisters, OR; Multnomah Books, 1995), 24-25.

Chapter Eight

1. Allen, *Getting Things Done*, 23.

Chapter Nine

1. Patti Chirico, "Calculating the High Cost of Clutter," Crown Financial Ministries, www.crown.org/Library/ViewArticle.aspx?ArticleId=448.

2. Ibid.

3. Ibid.

4. Seth Godin, "The inevitable decline due to clutter," *Seth Godin's Blog,* December 2, 2010, http://sethgodin.typepad.com/seths_blog/2010/12/the-inevitable-decline-from-clutter.html.

Chapter Ten

1. Allen, *Getting Things Done,* 62.

Chapter Twelve

1. "'Conventional Wisdom' vs. Current Ergonomics," Ankrum Associates, Workplace Ergo, Inc., http://office-ergo.com/current-ergo-thinking.

2. "Tips for Computer Users," UCLA Ergonomics, www.ergonomics.ucla.edu/Tips_Users.html.

Chapter Fourteen

1. Matt Richtel, "Growing Up Digital, Wired for Distraction," *New York Times*, November 21, 2010, sec. 1.

2. Eyal Ophir, Clifford Nass, and Anthony D. Wagner, "Cognitive control in media multitaskers," *Proceedings of the National Academy of Sciences*, 106, no. 33 (2009).

3. Jason M. Watson and David L. Strayer, "Supertaskers: Profiles in extraordinary multitasking ability," *Psychonomic Bulletin & Review* 17, no. 4 (2010): 479–485.

4. David Allen, *Ready for Anything* (New York: Penguin Group, 2003), 75.

Chapter Fifteen

1. Marla Cilley, "What is in a Shiny Sink?" FlyLady and Company, Inc., www.flylady.net/pages/shiny_sink_what.asp.

Chapter Sixteen

1. Star Lawrence, "Eat to Boost Mental Alertness," MedicineNet, Inc., www.medicinenet.com/script/main/art.asp?articlekey=56583.

Chapter Nineteen

1. Shari Braendel, "Autumn Closet Makeover," *P31 Woman*, October 2006, 5.

2. Monica Ricci, "Create Cash in Your Closet," HGTV, www.hgtv.com/organizing/create-cash-in-your-closet/index.html.

3. Eileen Koff, "Organizing Your Clothes Closet," *Everyday Life* (blog), Proverbs 31 Ministries, October 1, 2010, http://p31everydaylife.blogspot.com/2010/10/organizing-your-clothes-closet.html.

Chapter Twenty-One

1. Liberty Savard, *Shattering Your Strongholds* (Gainesville, FL: Bridge-Logos Publishers, 1992), 27.